THE MIND OF A LEADER

DECISIONS THAT IMPACT AND TRANSFORM

JAMES LASS

© **James Lass**

**James Lass
Guadalajara, Jalisco, Mexico
www.vivehoy.com.mx**

Dedication

To you, my beautiful wife, the beacon that illuminates my path with every step I take. Thank you for your unconditional love, your constant support, and for believing in my dreams even before I did.

To God and the universe, for guiding me, opening paths for me and reminding me every day that everything is possible when you act from the heart and faith.

To my wife's family, for their warm embrace and support at key moments. Their affection and trust have been a refuge and a strength.

To my fellow coaches, colleagues in this noble mission to transform lives. Together we build a world with more awareness, empathy, and purpose. Thank you for inspiring me to continue growing and learning.

And to all the people who have been there, big or small, visible or silent, know that your support has been a fundamental pillar on this path. This achievement is also his.

With infinite gratitude,

James Lass

PROLOGUE

Leadership is the ability to motivate, lead and change and has been studied from several aspects: thought, method, personality. But what happens in our hearts when we make decisions that change lives, businesses, and communities? What makes us the best leaders? In The Leader's Brain: Decisions Affecting Change and Change, we delve into the exciting area where neuroscience and leadership intersect and shed light on the scientific origins of our ability to influence and make good decisions.

This book is not a set of preconceived strategies or a magic formula for success. It is a detailed map of how the body that makes our decisions works, how it affects our emotions, and how we can use its great powers to become conscious, wise, and compassionate leaders. Here you'll learn why certain decisions are so important to your team, how to make neural connections to strengthen your problem-solving skills, and how to train your mind to be clear and articulate in an increasingly demanding world.

In my experience as a writer and expert in leadership development, I have discovered that great leaders are not born, but are formed by thinking, doing, and knowing. This book invites you to challenge limiting beliefs about leadership and dive into the tools modern science gives us to expand our abilities.

Get ready for a journey beyond the surface to the heart of what it means to be a leader. Mastermind will show you that by understanding and training your thoughts, you have the power to make decisions that not only affect, but change those around you.

On these pages you will find a collection of new ideas, practical examples and exercises designed for use in everyday life. It's more than just a book, it's an invitation to explore the infinite potential within you and become the leader you want to be.

This is your moment. Are you ready to lead with the power of your brain?

James Lass
NeuroLeadership Coach, Organizational Development, Executive and Business Coach

James Lass

Prologue — 5

Introduction — 11
- Leadership in the Age of Neuroscience — 11
- What is neuroleadership? — 17
- The Connection Between the Brain, Decision-Making, and Leadership — 20
- Why Understanding the Brain Is the Key to Leadership in the 21st Century — 23

Decisions That Make a Difference — 26
- The power of decisions in leadership. — 28
- What makes a decision transformative? — 34
- The impact of decisions on teams and organizations. — 40

How the Leader's Brain Works — 47
- Anatomy of the brain and its implications for leadership. — 50
- The prefrontal cortex: the center of conscious decisions. — 54
- Emotion, reason, and the struggle between the limbic system and the cortex. — 59

Emotions and their Role in Decision-Making — 63
- The role of emotional intelligence in leadership — 67
- How emotions influence our choices — 71
- Techniques to regulate emotions under pressure — 74

Neuroplasticity: How to Transform Your Mind to Lead Better — 83
- What is neuroplasticity and why does it matter? — 88
- Brain Training to Develop New Skills — 92

The growth mindset applied to leadership.	97
Decision-Making in Uncertainty Scenarios	**102**
How the brain processes risk and ambiguity	107
Neurological Strategies for Deciding in Critical Situations	111
The Importance of Confidence in Informed Intuition	116
Influence and Connection: Leading with Empathy	**120**
How the Brain Interprets and Responds to Social Connection	126
The Neuroscience of Empathy and Its Impact on Teams	131
Creating Psychologically Safe Environments	135
Stress Management and Leader Resilience	**141**
How Stress Affects the Brain and Decision-Making	145
Strategies for Staying Calm at Key Moments	150
Cultivating Resilience as a Leader	155
The Impact of Corporate Culture on the Brain	**160**
How the Environment Affects Our Neural Connections	165
Designing Organizational Cultures That Favor Growth	170
The Neuroscience of Recognition and Motivation	175
Innovation and Creativity in Leadership	**179**
The Relationship Between Neuroscience and Creativity	184
Techniques for Fostering Innovative Ideas in Teams	188
How to Get Out of Limiting Thought Patterns	192
Practical Tools for the Neuroconscious Leader	**197**
Exercises to Improve Decision Making	202
Techniques to Train Empathy and Emotional Regulation	208

Guide to Incorporating Neuroleadership into Everyday Life	213
The Future of Transformational Leadership	**218**
How Neuroleadership Redefines Success	223
The Next Steps to Lead with Purpose and Awareness	227
Final Inspiration	232
FINAL	236
About the Author	**242**

Page 10

INTRODUCTION
LEADERSHIP IN THE AGE OF NEUROSCIENCE

What do brains and leadership have in common? At first glance, it may not seem like much, but the truth is that the two are intimately related. The brain is the organ that allows us to think, feel, communicate, and act, and leadership is the ability to influence, motivate, and guide others toward a common goal. Therefore, knowing how the brain works and how it affects our behavior and that of others is essential to improve our leadership and that of our organizations.

Leadership is one of the most valued and in-demand skills in the world of work. However, it is not always exercised appropriately or adapted to the needs and expectations of employees. For this reason, neuroscience, the science that studies the brain and its relationship with behavior and cognition, is increasingly being used to better understand how the brains of leaders and workers work, and thus optimize their decision-making, communication, collaboration, learning, and change processes.

Neuroleadership is a discipline that arises from the union between neuroscience and leadership, and that seeks to apply scientific findings about the brain to organizational practices. According to David Rock and Jeffrey Swartz, two of the main references in this field, neuroleadership is based on the following principles

#1 **Every brain is unique**
You can't treat all employees the same, but you need to take into account their individual differences, preferences, strengths, and areas for improvement.

#2 **Reward systems are key**
The brain responds better to positive stimuli than to negative stimuli, so workers' recognition, feedback, autonomy and sense of purpose must be reinforced.

#3 There are no acts without emotions
The brain processes information emotionally rather than rationally, so the emotional climate of the organization must be taken care of, emotional intelligence and empathy must be fostered, and stress and fear must be avoided.

#4 The mind is programmed to cooperate
The brain is social and needs to interact with others to solve complex problems, so teamwork, trust, diversity, and inclusion should be promoted.

#5 Information influences expectations and behavior
The brain adapts to the reality it perceives, so clear, accurate and relevant information must be provided to employees, and ambiguity, uncertainty and misinformation must be avoided.

#6 The emotional state conditions actions

Page 12

The brain has a limited attention and memory span, so learning, creativity, and innovation should be facilitated, and overload, distraction, and routine should be avoided.

Neuroleadership has multiple benefits for organizations, as it contributes to improving the cohesion, motivation, satisfaction, adaptation and learning of work teams, which translates into greater productivity, quality, competitiveness and profitability. In addition, neuroleadership helps leaders develop their own capabilities, such as emotional intelligence, ease of learning, interest in workers, flexibility to adopt different leadership styles, a dialogic attitude, and negotiation skills.

Neuroleadership is a discipline in constant evolution, which is nourished by the advances of neuroscience, applying it to leadership, and the demands of the work environment. Therefore, leaders must be up to date with the latest research and trends, and apply them in a practical and personalized way to their contexts and objectives. Only then will they be able to take advantage of the full potential of their brains and that of their collaborators, and become neuroleaders.

When leaders make a difference

Leaders, identified by their ability to influence and direct others towards common goals, are individuals who drive and modify in a perceptible way the behavior of the group towards the achievement of its objectives, while promoting collaboration and voluntary commitment. Now, as it cannot be otherwise, they do not have to leave aside the emotional field. Daniel Goleman is a psychologist and author of one of his most recognized works, *Leadership: The Power of Emotional Intelligence*

(*Leadership. The Power of Emotional Intelligence*). In it he mentions 6 styles of leader, authoritarian, *coach*, conciliatory, democratic, exemplary and coercive (Goleman, 2014).

A new concept emerges: Neuroleadership

In line with several scholars, *neuroleadership* is defined as a tool that seeks to understand the processes of brain functioning in a broader way. In this way, it seeks to optimize performance in organizations and positively influence the organizational climate. To do this, it focuses on how individuals make decisions and solve problems in a social and work environment, as well as on the regulation of emotions and options for change.
A recent promise?
It should not be forgotten that *neuroleadership* represents a new conceptual dimension. Since it takes into account the development of the capacities of attention, concentration and emotional self-regulation essential in the modern leader. In this sense, he tries to define the neural basis of leadership and management.
Likewise, neurosciences study the procedures of the brain that explain the behavior reflected in the individual's performance, motivation, decision-making, emotional intelligence, the way of relating to others, and individual learning, among other aspects, linked to the organizational world and the exercise of leadership (Garzón et al., 2021).

Neuroscience and leadership
Within cognitive neuroscience, specifically based on leadership, social aspects have been highlighted. These

include decision-making, emotional regulation, influence and ease of generating change.

Aspects of leadership

With respect to decision-making, three factors are studied through cognitive neuroscience: stress, focus and clarity.

For example, there is brain imaging research that shows that high levels of stress cause the release of hormones that act as a defense mechanism against it. A change that leads to the active brain going into a *reflective* state.

Now, although this change is useful in critical situations, it can be unfavorable in leadership environments that involve high levels of stress, since it reduces cognitive abilities, and in extreme cases can configure the burnout syndrome. In accordance with the above, recent studies highlight how an individual's stress management can have a significant impact on improving their performance (Caballero & Gutiérrez, 2016).

Other social aspects

As mentioned above, when addressing the social aspects related to decision-making, it is critical to consider stress, focus, and clarity. However, it is important to remember that there are other social aspects that must also be taken into account in neuroleadership research.

Empathy, influence and change

In the case of emotional regulation in leaders, several studies have been carried out as a result of the relevance that regulation maintains when thinking. For Goleman (2014), being aware of one's own emotions and having empathy with other people affects relationship management. Consequently, activity is evident in the affective systems of the brain and in the control systems. Therefore, some emotional regulation strategies can generate better results than others.

On the other hand, **influence plays a fundamental role in leadership. This concept is related to the** principle of social reinforcement. Some authors highlight that monetary reinforcement mechanisms have the same weight as the stimulation obtained by social reinforcement, and can be highly pleasurable, generating positive effects on the performance of employees.

Finally, the ease of generating change, which is often influenced by the feeling of threat. However, throughout history, humans have created mechanisms to counter threats. At the brain level, warning signals are sent to the prefrontal cortex, and through thoughts and forms of behavior, adverse situations are resolved (Caballero & Gutiérrez, 2016).

What are the benefits of this?
First, it highlights an increase in efficiency when making decisions, which reduces the risk of selecting personnel not suitable for the position. On the other hand, the development of leadership skills is stimulated and creativity is increased.
In addition to the above, within *neuroleadership*, there are other benefits, since it promotes intrinsic motivation in employees. Thus, the theory of self-determination emphasizes that by satisfying needs for autonomy, competence and relationships, intrinsic motivation is stimulated. In addition, emotional leadership, by promoting a harmonious relationship, open communication, and support, meets these needs, also stimulating work commitment (Wan, et al., 2022).

Today, the focus is increasingly on the well-being of people within organizations. Thus, effective leaders not only influence the performance of employees, but also create healthier and more productive work environments. But is it enough to have developed cognitive and emotional skills, or are there other aspects to consider? The relationship between leadership and neuroscience invites us to explore beyond the surface and to question how we can fully harness the potential of the human brain in leadership.

WHAT IS NEUROLEADERSHIP?

Discover the secrets of good leadership and real change

Have you ever wondered what separates great leaders from great ones? It's not a theme, it's not an influence, it's not an event. It is something profound that each of us carries with us: the human brain and its extraordinary capacity for leadership and change.

Welcome to the world of neuroleadership, a revolutionary approach that combines neuroscience and leadership skills. Today I invite you to examine everything you know about leadership. We will challenge conventional rules and discover how you can develop your potential as a leader, not by instinct, but by understanding how your brain and that of others work.

Why is neuroleadership the future of leadership?
For years we were taught that leadership is a matter of skill: how to motivate a team, how to delegate, how to deal with problems. But here's a bold truth: The key to

leadership isn't in technology, but in a deep understanding of how the human mind works.

Neuroleadership teaches us that decision-making, emotions, and relationships are not mysterious. It's a brain process that you can learn to master and become a transformational leader. This knowledge not only empowers you, but also makes you a person who inspires, leads, and changes lives.
Stolen Leadership Myths Do you think leadership is genetic? Do only some people have "needs"?
Let me tell you something: those beliefs are chains that limit your true potential.

Neuroscience tells us that the human brain is plastic, which means it can change, grow, and change. In other words, it doesn't matter where you come from or how you started: you can become the leader you dream of.

The Incredible Benefits of Neuroleadership
Make Fast, Smart Decisions Do you sometimes feel paralyzed when faced with important decisions? Neuroleadership gives you the tools to learn how your brain works to make smarter, faster, and more effective decisions, even when you're under stress.

Empower and connect with your team to the next level
Learn how mirror neurons and brain empathy can help you create deeper, more meaningful relationships with your team, building trust and collaboration like never before.

Handle Stress Like a Pro
Did you know that you can rewire your brain to handle stress and turn it into a friend instead of an enemy? With

neuroleadership, you will turn these difficult moments into opportunities for growth.

Fostering Change and Change
In an ever-changing world, leaders must be agents of change. Neuroleadership teaches you how to adapt and lead your team to succeed in the midst of uncertainty.

Why do you need neuroleadership in your life?
This is not another fashion idea. It is an essential tool for leadership in the 21st century. It doesn't matter if you lead a small team, a large company, or just want to make a living. Neuroleadership is the bridge that connects your potential to what you want to have in the world.

But here's the thing: knowledge without action has no value. Today you have the opportunity to start changing the way you drive and live your life.

Now is the time to act
Every day is lost if you continue to lead without understanding the power of your brain. Don't let the opportunity to change your life and the lives of those around you be "one day."

Take the first step toward intentional, fulfilling, and transformative leadership. Neuroleadership is not just a tool, it is a change and you can be part of it.

Are you ready to let go of old beliefs and lead with a true purpose? The time to change your life and the lives of others starts now.

Try to lead like never before and find the power that has always been within you!

THE CONNECTION BETWEEN THE BRAIN, DECISION-MAKING, AND LEADERSHIP

The hidden power behind every decision

Have you ever wondered why some leaders seem to have the spiritual power to make decisions that impact and change? It's not luck or magic. This is neuroscience. I understand how the human brain works and use this knowledge to lead with purpose, clarity, and power. Today I invite you to explore how the relationship between your brain and decision-making can be the key to taking your leadership to the next level.

Challenging Common Beliefs in Leadership
For many years, we have believed that leadership is based on technical skills or achievements. However, it's not just leadership that controls work, but also understanding the engine that drives all decisions: the brain.

Your brain is the most advanced organ in the known world, but here's the thing: most people use it on autopilot. They act but don't react, make quick decisions, and let their emotions get the best of them. What would you think if I told you that you could program autopilot to become a great leader? What if you didn't just make a decision, but inspired meaningful change?

The Science of Challenging Independence

There are two main parts of the brain that influence leadership decisions:

Limbic system: Responsible for our thoughts, feelings, and needs.

Prefrontal cortex: Responsible for data analysis, processing, and decision-making.

Amazing things happen when these two parts work together: decision-making and smart support. This balance will not only change the way you lead, but also the way others see you.

A real-life example

Think of a boss you really admire. Why does this happen? Perhaps it's your ability to organize your thoughts while making smart decisions. This is not an accident. This is a direct result of understanding how the brain works and using it as a powerful tool.

Surprising benefits of this method

Fast and effective decision-making: Knowing when to trust your gut and when to follow it will save you time and energy.

Build closer connections with your team: By understanding what's happening in meetings, you can create an environment of trust and motivation.

Stress management: Learning to control your brain can help you stay calm and clear even in the most difficult of times. This
is not just an idea; it is an applied science. Here's the best part: you can learn how to do it.

Your heart is your best assistant

Transformational leadership starts with you. But here's the truth that many people avoid saying: If you haven't learned to lead yourself, you won't be able to lead others. This means understanding how your brain works, eliminating negative beliefs, and improving your decision-making.

The good news is that you don't need to be psychic to use it. With the right knowledge and tools, you can uncover clues that will change your life, starting with yourself.

Page 22

James Lass

WHY UNDERSTANDING THE BRAIN IS THE KEY TO LEADERSHIP IN THE 21ST CENTURY

Did you know that a successful leader in the 21st century isn't just about leading a team or making good decisions? These are the ones who understand how the human brain works, whether it's yours or your team's. The 21st century is changing the way we understand leadership and if you don't understand how the brain works, you'll be left behind. I invite you on a journey into the future of leadership. Are you ready to find out why understanding your brain is an incredible power that will transform your leadership skills?

Assessing Common Beliefs About Leadership
For centuries, leadership has been misdefined: as quick decision-making, skill, and authority. However, this capacity is no longer sufficient in this century. Today, effective leadership is tied to a deeper understanding of how the human brain works. The brain not only controls our emotions, but also our responses to problems, the decisions we make, and the way we relate to others.

The problem is that most leaders don't realize how their decisions affect their team's morale. Worse, their leadership skills ignore the impact of their emotions and brain responses.

The Brain: The Secret Source of Good Leadership
Here's the truth: The human brain is the key to everything. And leaders who don't understand how to use

The Mind of a Leader

that knowledge limit their ability to change, inspire, and transform. Good decisions don't come from the mind alone; They are born from a combination of well-managed emotions, proper intuition, and a deep understanding of how to create better neural networks in every situation.

This is what makes the difference between great leaders. It doesn't matter how many years of experience you have or how many strategies you know; This is how you will be able to understand and manage your emotions, impulses, and the actions of your brain and others to make decisions that will change everything around you.

Surprising Benefits of Understanding Your Brain
Smarter, Faster Decision-Making: Understanding your brain helps you make the right decision in a situation, without being held back by emotions and stress.
Better connections and connections: By understanding how your partner's brain works, you can create deeper, clearer connections that align with your vision.
Strong endurance: A well-trained brain can handle obstacles, doubts, and setbacks. Being a leader in the 21st century means staying in power when the world stops.
Stay inspired: Knowing how to create the right network within yourself and your team gives you the power to stay motivated and motivated, creating more and more teams.
What 21st century leaders know... And you can learn more
Great leaders in any field are bad communicators. They know how to make people think, feel, and behave differently. But it's not magic, it's science. You, as a future leader, need to know this knowledge.
The neuroscience behind leadership is available to

everyone, but few use it. Do you want to be a part of acquiring this knowledge, or will others be left behind on the path to a better future?

It's time to work

Today you have a special opportunity: use your brainpower to become an outstanding leader. This is the difference between emotional leadership and interpersonal communication. Leaders of the 21st century are writing the rules of the game, and now is the time to join them.

If you always think you need more experience or skills, you're holding yourself back. The real question is: are you ready to change direction? The only way to achieve this is to understand how your team's brains and your team work. And don't just listen, use it to your advantage.

The days of traditional leaders are over. The era of neuroleaders has begun.

DECISIONS THAT MAKE A DIFFERENCE

Decision-making: the power of deliberate choice

We make decisions every day. From what to eat for breakfast to how to answer unexpected questions. But there is a truth that few accept: not all decisions are created equal. There are unknown decisions and life-changing decisions. What decision are you making today?

The question is not whether you make a decision, but whether you make the right decision. It changes, creates and characterizes the before and after. Because let me tell you something: success is not about being lucky, it's the direct result of the decisions you make every day.

Evaluation of common beliefs about decisions
Many believe that important decisions are made only in difficult situations. But the situation is different: small decisions have big consequences. Life is not defined by one or two moments, but by thousands of micro-shots each day.

Take on a new challenge or stay in your comfort zone?
Should I speak at this meeting or remain silent?
Delay progress or take the first step towards real change?

Many people despise their freedom of choice, because they believe that the Scriptures are written. It's time to fight that belief! You have the power to choose, and your decisions are the blueprint for your future.

Page 26

The results of voluntary decision-making. It's not just an idea; It is knowledge. Our brains are designed to adapt and change based on the choices we make. All decisions work on a nervous system that reinforces competence, confidence and the ability to face problems.

Smart Decisions:

Unwavering self-confidence: When you make good decisions, you become someone who knows what you want and how to get it.
Growth: Smart decisions that take you out of your comfort zone and take you to new levels of success.
True Relationships: By choosing your values, you attract people who share your vision and energy.
Decision Making Game
Think of your favorite person. A leader, a visionary, an entrepreneur. Do you think they suddenly got to where they were? They did NOT come because they made hard, courageous, and often unpopular decisions. The decision forced them to leave their comfort zone, but it meant their lives.

And here's the interesting part: you can do the same.

What decision will change your life today?
The important question is not whether you can change your life; The question is: are you ready to make the decisions that will make this happen? Maybe it's time to invest in yourself, say yes to opportunities that scare you, or let go of things that aren't right for you.

Because let's face it: every day you delay a decision, you lose time and opportunities. There is no better time. Now is the time to act.

It's time to make a decision

This is not just a call to think. This is a straightforward question for you. Don't wait for life to decide for you and make a decision. Because the decision you make today will be tomorrow's story.

Choose the size. Select the variables. Choose to make a decision that will make a difference.

THE POWER OF DECISIONS IN LEADERSHIP.

The Power of Decision-Making and Leadership: The Art of Changing Every Choice

There comes a time in every leader's life when everything stops. Right now, we face decisions that can determine not only our path, but also the course of those who trust us. Sad truth: leadership is used in names or words, but with the ability to make decisions that influence and change.

Decision-making explained by leaders

Many people believe that leadership is about grace, experience, or strength. But what happens if the results don't come? When is the group not developing? The problem is not strategy or talent. This is because these decisions were not made out of fear or doubt.

Effective leadership is a skill, its basis is determination. Every choice, from how to handle conflict to how to move forward, sends the message, "Believe me, I know where we're going" with wisdom. Admitting that you don't have all the answers and looking for a relationship is one of the most powerful decisions you can make.

Belief: "The faster, the better"
Fact: It's not about speed, it's about accuracy. Confident leaders know when to act quickly and when to wait because they understand that speed affects the quality of decisions.

Affirmation: "It's better to make strong decisions"
Truth: Yes, not every decision will please everyone. But good leaders choose honesty and a long-term perspective that ultimately builds respect and trust.

The Amazing Impact of Decisive Leaders
Leaders who make courageous and decisive decisions make a difference:

Group change in society: decisions aligned with values that inspire commitment. People don't just work for those leaders; They join them.

Innovation : When team members see leaders taking calculated risks, they feel empowered to do the same.
Building lasting trust: Decisions that destroy trust, even if they are difficult, strengthen it;

Every decision you make as a leader is a seed planted in the soil of the future. What are you cultivating today with your choices?

The Leader's Brain: Decision-Making Leaders
The science of leadership is closely related to how our brains process information. Neuroleadership teaches us that the best decisions do not come from instinct or external pressure, but from a mind trained to observe, reflect and act systematically.

Purposeful decision-making activates parts of the brain associated with accuracy and confidence.
It measures risk and reward, strengthening the connection between emotion and logic, creating a perfect balance.
The main thing is to train your mind to see beyond the visible, to turn difficulties into opportunities and, most importantly, to act without fear.

It's time to decide on a change of leadership. It requires leaders who have the courage to make decisions despite uncertainty. Because every difficult decision means a step towards change and every right choice means change.

The question is: can you lead well? The question is: What decision will you make that could change everything?

Today is the time to act. If you lead for no reason, you lead blindly. But when you lead with purpose, you make a lasting impact.

Choose to be the leader your team, your organization, and the world want. Let your decision be a legacy. Because every leader who dares to make a decision about goals and visions has the ability to change not only today, but also the future of those around them.

The Power of Decision-Making in Leadership: In short, leadership is the act of making decisions. From childhood to adulthood, all leaders face a roadmap: where are we going and how will we get there? Understanding the consequences of our decisions not only changes the direction of the organization, but also impacts our leadership and our lives.

Ethical Choices
As a leader, every decision you make sends a message to your team. People focus on your decisions and how you make them.

Do you have access or control? Chapter Are You Strong or Not? Is your choice fear or luck? When you make clear and objective decisions, you create a culture of trust and loyalty. But if you procrastinate, avoid, or act too quickly, the results will be uncertain and unreliable.

Working Groups: Decision-Making and Leadership
Decision-making doesn't just happen in the head; It's an interesting balance between emotion, feeling, and experience.

Emotion as the main driver:
All decisions begin with an emotional response. This is a warning sign that you need something. Their problem? Don't let this emotion be your only driving force.

Balance of reason and emotion:

The Mind of a Leader

Effective leaders know how to combine logic with reason. This is where cognitive training comes in: it's a well-organized mind that connects what it hears with what it knows and turns data and insights into action.

Repetition makes perfect:
Every thought you have trains your brain to do this. When you make the right decisions, your leadership becomes a powerful "muscle."

The cost of not choosing:
Many times, the biggest enemy of leadership is not bad decisions, but bad thinking. Not to choose is to choose:

I choose to stand.
I let others take responsibility
Send malicious messages to your group.
In a changing environment, downtime is the quickest and least necessary option.
Difference between ordinary and special decisions
Not all decisions are created equal. Many people solve problems quickly; Surprise changes reality.

Common option: focus on the important things and always forget about the important things.
Concrete choices: Consider the purpose, long-term impact, and legacy that will guide you.
Leaders who want to excel are not afraid of difficult decisions. They know that they are the most important place to grow, innovate and create something lasting.

How to Make Decisions That Benefit and Change
Define your purpose:

All decisions should be aligned with your needs and goals. If you don't know what it stands for, your options will be limited.

Analyze the risk, but don't rest:
Analysis is important, but don't let perfection get in the way of progress. Sometimes the best decision is to settle for what you have.

Listen, but lead:
Giving back is important, but ultimately, you are responsible. The owner has the right to choose, but not the right to decide.

Train your brain to make better decisions:
Meditation, continuous learning, and life experience develop your ability to make decisions under pressure.
Learn from mistakes:
Even bad decisions can be beneficial if you use them to grow and change your path.

Choice and Change: The Call to Be a Leader
Leadership doesn't mean having all the answers. Moving forward with purpose, building trust, and making decisions can lead to change. In all decisions, you have the power to change your circumstances and you have the power to change yourself.

The question is: Are you ready to be a leader who makes big decisions? Because leadership does not wait for important places. It is time to act, to choose, to change.

WHAT MAKES A DECISION TRANSFORMATIVE?

What will the decision change?

During our lifetime, we make thousands of decisions, from what to eat for breakfast to how we do our jobs. But have you ever stopped to think about what makes a decision be made? We're not talking about small decisions every day, but ones that change the game, define your path, and inspire your potential.

I invite you to know your opinion on decision-making. Are you ready to discover the hidden power behind transformative decisions and how you can start using them to change your life today?

History of important decisions
We were taught that to make important decisions we must analyze every last detail, see all the possible results and wait for "the perfect moment". Let me tell you: that moment will never come.

The decision to change is not about having all the answers, but about understanding who you are and where you want to go. Along with perfectionism, the most important thing is to commit to progress.

Page 34

"It's not the decision to eliminate some problem that makes the decision to change, but the one that connects you to your deepest purpose."

What will the decision change?
In scientific terms, change decisions are recognized by activating the main parts of the brain related to reality, long-term vision, and internal motivation. Let's look at the most important things:

1. *Clear goals*
The decision to change starts with a solid foundation: knowing what you really want.
The frontal lobe, which is responsible for planning and thinking, functions when we see a clear goal. Without clear direction, our decisions are scattered and ineffective.

Change your life: Ask yourself, will this choice bring me closer to the life I want to create? If the answer isn't "yes," it's time to reconsider.

2. *Courage to face change*
Change creates uncertainty, and our brain, especially the amygdala, can interpret it as a threat. That's why most people stay in their comfort zone that prevents them from growing.

The decision to change challenges you to face fear with courage. It's not the lack of fear that changes the outcome, but your ability to act independently.
Change your life: friends only if. Know that it's a sign that you're about to cross the line and take it to the next level.

3. Influence yourself and others

Changing decisions will not only change your life; It will have a gentle effect on the people around you. When you make decisions based on your values, you inspire others to do the same.

Neuroscientist Antonio Damasio discovered that emotions are very important in decision-making. Not only will you be driven to make decisions based on your positive feelings, but it will also affect those around you.

Change your life: Ask yourself, how will this decision affect the people I love and lead?

4. Consent to act

A clear decision is a matter of no consequence. This is where your dopaminergic system comes into play: dopamine, also known as the stimulant molecule, is released when you do something specific to your goals.

Practice, no matter how small, boosts your confidence and creates a healthy progression pattern.

Change your life: Break down your decisions into clear steps and execute every action. This will give you a lot.

The current time is

The change decision is not waiting for a full condition. It does not stop the "what do they say" and the fear of failure. Serious, defiant and a good person.

Today I challenge you to ask yourself this question:

What decision will I make that can change my life?

Page 36

You don't need a path of fire; You have to work hard for yourself. Because transformative decisions don't just change your time: they define your future and the legacy you leave behind.

Big mistake: thinking that all decisions are the same
We've been told that "making decisions is part of life." What they don't tell us is that all decisions are different.

The biggest mistake we make is to believe that all options have the same value. Deciding what to wear to a meeting is nothing compared to deciding whether to leave a job you don't like, move to another country, or start your dream business. There is one important thing when making the decision to change something: it is not easy. They take you out of your comfort zone and that's why they lure you to greatness.
"True leadership starts when you make a bold decision, not a good one."

What makes you decide to change your life?
To understand how a decision can truly change, we need to go beyond the obvious. Here we enter the fascinating area of the human brain and its relationship with leadership and decision-making.

1. Align with your internal goals
The decision to change is practical and irrational; It's very emotional. Research in neuroscience shows that the brain makes important decisions based not only on logic (frontal cortex), but also on emotions (limbic system).

When you make a decision about your goals, you use your brain's power to propel you forward even when things are tough. A combination of goals makes effective and impactful decisions.

How do you do that?
Take the time to think about your values, your deepest goals, and what's important to you. When you make a decision about it, you will feel an unstoppable power.

2. The Power of Calculated Risk
The decision to change may be risky, but not clear. In fact, neuroscience research has shown that moderate levels of uncertainty activate areas of the brain associated with learning and adaptation.

Truth: The fear of failure will always be there. But so is the opportunity to improve. The people who have left their mark on the world are not those who avoid danger, but those who face it with strategy.

What are you going to do?
Ask yourself before making a big decision: What could possibly go wrong? And most importantly, what's the best thing that could happen to me if I make this decision?

3. Create a positive ripple effect
Decisions that not only affect your life; They have the power to change the behavior of the people around you. Think of it this way: when a manager commits to creating a positive workplace, they improve the quality of their entire team. When you choose to take care of your emotional health, you encourage others to do the same.

The decisions you make have consequences. Therefore, any decision to change is also a management decision.

Practical action: Consider how your choices affect others. Think about the impact you can have if you choose truth, courage, and vision. . Neuroscience tells us that every small step toward a goal releases dopamine, the brain chemical associated with motivation and pleasure. These products boost your self-confidence and make you feel better.

The key to success:

Break down your decisions into concrete steps.
Enjoy every achievement, no matter how small.
Shikama. Change doesn't happen overnight, but every day matters.
Position accuracy: what decisions are you procrastinating?
Think about it: every decision you make builds your future, whether it's the path to your goals and your success or your relationship.

Today I invite you to take a closer look at the decisions you have made. You know who he is. What you feel inside can change your life, but it scares you because you know it's important.

What are you waiting for? More people? The real clue here is: yourself.

Do not save again. Tomorrow is not the time to make that decision you left, but now. Because in the end life is not measured by the opportunities we are given, but by the decisions we make to achieve them.

You have a choice. Have the courage to change. Because the true power of a leader, a visionary and influence is not in what he knows, but in the decisions he wants to make.

THE IMPACT OF DECISIONS ON TEAMS AND ORGANIZATIONS.

The Impact of Decisions on Teams and Organizations

In the world of leadership, there's one fact you can't forget: the decisions you make not only influence the direction of your journey, they also change the lives of everyone around you. But to what extent do we understand the impact of our decisions on our teams and our organizations?

Today is the day to break away from your small beliefs, look beyond the obvious, and see how this can make or break your legacy as a leader.

Big Cartel: Decision-Making Is Just a Matter of Logic
How many times have you heard that decisions should be "thoughtful"? The reality is that the decisions teams and organizations make are both emotional and strategic.

Page 40

Neuroscience backs this up: our brains don't really separate emotions from logic when making decisions.

This is not a weakness; This is strong. When you understand the emotional impact of the decisions you make, you don't just change the numbers, you also change people. And in leadership, talent is key.

Domino Reactions: How One Decision Changes Everything
Every decision in an organization has a ripple effect. Consider:

Leaders who choose to invest in the emotional health of their teams experience increased productivity and loyalty. A bad decision, such as ignoring an employee's concerns, can destroy trust and morale in a matter of weeks.
This is the real challenge: knowing that elections can be a good start or can be the first step towards chaos.

What makes a decision effective?
Not all decisions are created equal. To make decisions that change groups and organizations, three criteria must be met:

1. *Understanding the Program*
Sound decisions answer a fundamental question: Why do we do this?

Effective leaders don't make decisions for the sake of making decisions. Every choice they make is aligned with a clear vision and goals. According to research in management psychology, teams that understand the "why" behind decisions experience a 20% increase in engagement.

2. Benefits of positive emotions

The human brain is designed to respond to emotions. When your decisions are inspiring, motivating, and rewarding, employees will not only do their jobs, they will work harder.

It's not about avoiding difficult decisions. This means speaking to them with compassion and showing them that every choice, no matter how difficult, has a greater purpose.

3. Continuous action

This is not only a decision, but also an implementation. Decisions that have a real impact must be translated into concrete and measurable actions. A study by Harvard Business Review shows that 70% of failed decisions are not due to the decision being made poorly, but because it was poorly implemented.

The decision to form a team of merit

Do you want to build a team that follows your orders, but shares your vision? Here are three important decisions for changing your equipment:

1. Commitment to talent development

Deciding to invest in training and grow your team is a safe choice. When employees understand that their personal development is important, their performance and productivity will increase.

2. Create a culture of trust

By deciding to make actions and decisions clear, trust develops. Trust is the foundation of every successful team.

3. Improve overall health

Decisions to protect your team's physical and mental health can not only reduce stress, but also increase creativity and energy.

Decisions that change organizations

Now, let's look at the macro level: What kind of decisions affect the organization as a whole?

1. Bold innovation

Successful organizations aren't afraid to make risky, creative decisions. If you stay in your comfort zone, you'll be left behind.

2. Strategy Strategy

The world is changing rapidly and successful organizations are those that decide to adapt quickly. It doesn't have to be sudden, but it does require a quick turnaround.

3. Personal leadership

The most successful companies are not only profitable; They seek influence. A commitment to leadership and purpose motivates employees and customers.

The decisions you make as a leader aren't just binary choices. It is a transformative process that has the power to create culture, motivate teams and set the course for the entire organization. But the true magnitude of this power is unknown. Now is the time to change that.

Imagine a team where each member feels that their contribution is important, trust flows like a river, and is evident in all activities. Now imagine the opposite. Teams paralyzed by lack of direction, exhausted by uncertainty, disappointed by unmotivated leaders. What's the difference between the two? It's your decision.

The absolute power of decisions

Every decision, no matter how small, creates a ripple effect. From everyday conversations in meetings to high-level business strategies, everything has consequences. But this is a secret. The right decisions aren't the only things that really make a difference. They are brave people.

Science teaches that the human brain is a complex machine designed to prevent damage. The amygdala warns us of danger and the frontal cortex helps us think. But leadership involves much more than the decision-making process. It means connecting logic and emotion with leadership and design.

The role of decisions in successful teams

1. Decisions that improve confidence

Trust is the glue that holds teams together. When you decide to be transparent, show love, and keep your promises, the results are amazing. A study conducted by the Great Place to Work Institute found that highly engaged teams are 50% more productive and have 76% lower turnover rates.

2. Decisions that promote cooperation

Teams that believe their leaders value diversity of opinion are more creative and resilient. Making the decision to invite everyone to the table, listen carefully and act on it will not only foster creativity but also a sense of belonging.

3. Decide to exercise human rights
Never underestimate the power of a kind word or public recognition. The decision to value people for who they are, not just what they do, creates a respectful and motivating work environment.

Change organizations according to their purpose
Organizations are not abstract entities. A living ecosystem is created through everyday decisions. Like any other ecosystem, its health depends on the actions of the people who lead it.

1. Decide with a purpose, not just for profit.
Successful companies in the 21st century are those that understand that financial success is an outcome, not a goal. When you choose to lead and be creative, you inspire your employees, customers, and the community at large.

2. Able to innovate despite risk
In an ever-changing world, adaptability is a risky good. Bold decisions that defy convention are what will keep you organized and competitive.

3. Decide to adapt quickly.
Agility in management is not something isolated, it is necessary. The decision to adjust strategy, adopt new technology, or reorganize teams is what differentiates successful companies from those that survive.

The science behind the new decisions
Did you know that every time you make a decision, you're rewiring your brain? This is due to neuroplasticity, the brain's ability to create and adjust synaptic connections in response to experience.

Your brain is trained to be a more effective leader as you make decisions based on compassion, logic, and reason. And here's the best part. You're also influencing the brains of those around you. A study published in Frontiers in Human Neuroscience found that leaders who make clear and positive decisions activate neural circuits in their team, creating cohesion and trust.

Time to make a decision: change starts with you.
Ignorance is the greatest enemy of effective leadership. Every day you postpone a decision, every day you doubt your leadership ability, you miss an opportunity to change your team and your organization.

There is no limit to the impact of your decisions. This can increase the equipment to its full potential or reduce it to inefficiency. But this is the truth. You have the right to choose.

Do you sit back and walk away for fear of making a mistake? Will you take office, take responsibility, and lead with confidence?

Page 46

James Lass

HOW THE LEADER'S BRAIN WORKS

When we talk about leadership, we often think of intelligence, charisma or ability to influence. But what if I told you that the real power behind a leader isn't their character or their experience, but something deeper? The brain.

Leadership does not begin in a chat room nor is it associated with a leader's name. It starts with the neural connections in the brain. This wonderful body that weighs more than a kilo is responsible for every decision, every thought, and every impact you create on your team and on your team. Can you imagine what you could achieve if you knew how to improve your work?

Get ready to discover the secrets of guided thoughts and how you can use them to change not only your life but everyone's life.

Pure faith: leadership is not intelligence, it is neuroscience
Forget the stories that leaders are born with a "special gift." Leadership is not a basic skill, it is a basic skill. How? Use neuroplasticity, the brain's ability to adapt and create new synaptic connections in response to experience, learning, and challenges.

For example, every time you manage conflicts, make good decisions, or motivate your team, you retrain your brain to be more efficient.

And here's a fact that defies everything you think you know: The leader's brain doesn't work the same way the average brain does. Leadership requires a unique combination of skills that requires:

Fast and effective decision-making.
Empathy connects with others, long-term vision of hope and problem solving.

Leadership Research: Your Brain in Action

1. Amygdala: Guardian of Safety
The amygdala is the part of the brain responsible for our emotions, especially fear. As a leader, it's important to learn how to control this "alarm center." When you control your fear, you'll be able to make sound decisions and act clearly even in the midst of chaos.

2. Prefrontal cortex: the center of good decision-making
The brain area is the center of thinking, planning, and decision-making. The more you develop your prefrontal cortex with challenges, learning, and thinking, the better it will function. This creates great ideas and concepts.

3. Reward system: intrinsic motivation
Have you ever felt depressed after achieving a goal? This is because the brain's reward system releases dopamine, a motivational motivator. Successful leaders know how to activate this system not only within themselves but also within their organizations.
. Big decisions
Organization-changing decisions are not made out of convenience, but out of courage. Effective leaders train their brains to avoid uncertainty and make decisions.

How to achieve it? Always expose yourself to new situations and learn from them, even if you fail.

Intentional Love
Neuroscience shows that compassion is not just a feeling; It is also poisonous. It activates your brain's "mirror nerves" so you can connect with your team's thoughts and feelings. This not only builds trust, but also encourages collaboration and innovation.

Strategic Thinking
A leader's mind is like radar: it is always looking for patterns, anticipating challenges and providing solutions. This should teach your mind to look beyond the immediate problem and focus on the bigger picture.

Change starts in your brain
Here's a big revelation: You don't have to wait to become the leader you've always dreamed of. Your brain already has everything it needs to do this. All you need is to learn how to use their ideas.

Some activities you can start today:
Meditation: Meditation activates the body first and reduces the activity of the amygdala, allowing you to be positive and clear.
Continuous learning: Each new experience creates new connections, improving your ability to solve complex problems.
Give thanks: This simple act releases dopamine and strengthens relationships, which is essential for good leadership.

Your brain, your power

The Mind of a Leader

Your brain is the most powerful tool you have as a leader. It can inspire, change and lead people to the best. But here's the key: you have to decide to open it.

Today you have the opportunity to become a leader who not only leads, but changes lives. Your brain is ready for the challenge. And you?

Don't wait any longer. Start training your mind, challenge your limits, and use your greatest asset: a leader's brain.

ANATOMY OF THE BRAIN AND ITS IMPLICATIONS FOR LEADERSHIP.

Leadership is not an acquired skill or a quality possessed by a privileged few. This ability is closely related to the structure and function of our brain. From how we process information to how we respond to stress, the anatomy of the brain holds the key behind the fundamental decisions and moments of inspiration that define some of history's original value-changers.

Today we will explore how the magnificent biological machine, the brain, defines a leader's style, performance, and vision. But be careful: what you're about to discover will forever change the way you think about leadership... and yourself.

Neurorevolution in Leadership

For years we have thought of leadership as a value, idea or experience. But neuroscience shows something deeper and more powerful: At the heart of leadership is a distinctive dance of different nervous systems.

Theoretical knowledge is not enough to lead change; You need to understand how your brain works and how to teach it to improve your ability to motivate, make decisions, and connect.

Fundamentals of Leadership in the Brain

The human brain has more than 86 billion neurons divided into specific regions that play an important role in leadership. Here's how these areas affect your leadership skills:

1. Prefrontal Cortex: Expert Expert
The prefrontal cortex is the control center of the brain. This is where decision-making, planning, and thought management occur. Leaders with a functional mind and a balanced prefrontal cortex can:

solve difficult problems clearly.
Consider the long term when managing current priorities.
Stay calm and instill confidence in the team.
However, chronic stress can affect your work. This means that learning to manage stress is not a luxury, but an important part of thinking.

2. Limbic system: the engine of depression

The limbic system includes structures such as the amygdala and hippocampus, which are responsible for our thoughts and memories. In terms of leadership, this system defines your ability to:

Read your team's thoughts and respond with understanding.
It builds trust and inspires others.
Control your thoughts and don't get caught up in negative thoughts.
A balanced limbic allows you to be guided by understanding and connection, without falling into critical or fear-based decisions.

3. Mirror neurons: research links
Have you ever seen how a leader's passion spreads to his team? This is thanks to mirror neurons, which are responsible for perception and action. These neurons provide:

Your thoughts and behaviors directly affect your organization's culture.
You inspire others by having confidence and determination.
You create a collaborative and collaborative environment.
Emotionally conscious leaders prefer commitment and loyalty.

4. Basal Core: The Art of Constant Action
The basal ganglia are the driving force behind behavior and automatic behavior. When it comes to leadership, they play an important role in:

Create effective processes that will increase your productivity.

Developing a consistent attitude can boost your confidence.

Ability to rely on pressure.
If you've ever wondered why some people work without energy, the answer usually lies in the strength of their personality, i.e., brain image.

Challenge: Do you bring your whole brain with you?
Most leaders operate on autopilot, unaware of how their brain structure influences every action, interaction, and outcome. But here's the bold truth: exceptional leadership requires extraordinary minds.

The good news is that you can train your brain to be more efficient, objective, and connected. Here are some practical tips:

Prioritize your face: Practice mindfulness to improve your ability to focus and manage your thoughts.

Evaluate your limbic system: Take some time to think about your personality traits and how they impact your team.

Activate your mirror neurons: Create effective communication skills and inspire others by example.
Optimizing your core ganglia: Identify and reinforce habits that bring you closer to your leadership goals.

The brain as the secret weapon of the leader of the 21st century
Understanding how the brain works is not a scientific curiosity; This is the key to unlocking your true leadership potential.

The Mind of a Leader

Consider every decision with confidence, empower your team, and achieve results that will change their lives. This is not an unrealizable ideal; It's the direct result of learning to align your thoughts with your goals.

Science is on your side, but action is on your side. Don't wait any longer and check the influence of your brain on your leaders. Change starts here and now. Are you ready to reach your potential?

THE PREFRONTAL CORTEX: THE CENTER OF CONSCIOUS DECISIONS.

What's the first thing that comes to mind when you think about an important decision in your life? Current stress? Fear of action? Maybe you feel clarity when everything seems to fall into place. But what you don't think about is the real characteristic behind all good decisions: your thoughts.

Page 54

The part of the brain behind the forehead is not the only living part of the body. He is your inner planner, your moral compass, and the architect of your greatest dreams. It allows you not only to respond to life, but also to create it. In this blog, we'll explore this brain center and how you can use it to transform your leadership, your emotions, and your life.

Prefrontal Cortex: An Evolutionary Miracle
The prefrontal cortex (PFC) is the product of millions of years of evolution and is one of the most unique features of the human brain. It makes up a small part of the brain, but it consumes the wrong amount of energy: about 20 percent of the entire brain. This shows its importance.

The PFC is associated with higher cognitive functions, which leads us to identify:

Psychological Decision Making: Selection of multiple options based on reflection and analysis.
Long-term planning: Thinking about goals and planning the steps needed to achieve them.
Impulse management: Respond to immediate challenges and be confident in future benefits.

Compassion and Ethics: Considering the interests of others when making decisions.
But this powerful weapon has a fatal weakness: stress, fatigue, and lack of training can damage it.

The power to predict decisions
Have you ever wondered why some people make the wrong decisions over and over again? It is not luck or a force of nature; The result is a well-trained CPF.

The Mind of a Leader

Most of us make sudden decisions without thinking. This is because other parts of the brain, such as the limbic system (responsible for emotions), need to be under control during times of stress. While emotions are important, relying solely on them can lead to overreaction and an inability to make informed decisions.

Then CPF is your secret tool. It allows you to take a step back, evaluate your options, and choose the option that works best for you and others, not just the easiest or most fun option.

How the Prefrontal Cortex Works
To understand its function, we must first study how it works.

1. Information integration
The PFC acts as a central processing unit, integrating information from different parts of the brain. Let's say you're looking for a job opportunity:

Your limbic system tells you how the job opportunity makes you feel (emotionally).
Your parietal brain analyzes numerical data (perception).
Your memory recalls past experiences in the same activity. The CPF
It brings it all together to help you make a sound and informed decision.

2. Future policy
CPF as a pregnancy simulator. It allows you to imagine future situations, calculate risks, and predict outcomes. This ability to plan for the long term is the key to success in any area of your life.

Page 56

However, this prediction is not always true. Today, many people live in the trap of letting their emotions guide their decisions.

3. Impulse control
In a world full of distractions, the CPF is a safeguard against temptation. It helps you say "no" to things that don't serve your purpose and focus on what's important.

Leaders with a strong CPF know how to prioritize, ignore the noise, and focus on what matters.

Provident and Leadership Fund
When we talk about leadership, the Provident Fund plays an important role. Here are some of the ways in which influence manifests:

1. Principled decision-making
Wise leaders evaluate not only outcomes, but also how decisions affect people. CPF helps align immediate benefits with long-term impact, ensuring actions are aligned with core values.

2. Protection from stress
Stress blocks the prefrontal cortex, causing us to make poor decisions. Leaders who practice mindfulness and other emotion regulation techniques keep their prefrontal cortex active even in times of high stress.

3. Conflict resolution
Trained CPF leaders can manage conflict through compassion and strategy rather than reacting aggressively or avoiding problems.

How to Train Your Prefrontal Cortex

If the prefrontal cortex is so powerful, why don't we make the most of it? The answer is simple: you need training. Here are some neuroscience-based reinforcement strategies:

1. Mindfulness Practice
Mindfulness reduces activity in the limbic system and strengthens connections with the prefrontal cortex. Spend 10 minutes each day meditating or focusing on your breathing.

2. Regular Exercise
Exercise increases blood flow to the brain and improves PFC function. Aerobic exercise such as jogging or walking works well.

3. Stimulate your mind
Solving problems, learning new skills, and reflecting on your decisions can strengthen neural connections in the prefrontal cortex.

4. Prioritize sleep
PFCs often have trouble sleeping. Make sure you get at least 7-8 hours of sleep every day to maintain optimal performance.

Your future is in your hands... Not only your prefrontal cortex, it's the source of your power. Leadership, motivation, and change require decision, and this depends on how well you train this part of your brain.

Imagine what you could achieve if every decision you made was aligned with your values and goals. Imagine

Page 58

leading with clarity, purpose, and an unstoppable ability to inspire others.

The leader's mind is not exposed; it is a crop. Start your CPF training today and unleash your true potential. Your life, your decisions, and the people you lead deserve better.

EMOTION, REASON, AND THE STRUGGLE BETWEEN THE LIMBIC SYSTEM AND THE CORTEX.

There is a constant battle within you, a dance between two powerful forces that shape your every decision: the limbic system and the cerebral cortex. One is the steward of your thoughts; But what happens when these forces collide? This invisible struggle not only determines your decisions, but also determines the path of your life.

If you've ever felt like your heart wants something, but your mind tells you otherwise, you've experienced this battle of brains. In this blog, we'll look at how it works, how it affects your leadership, and most importantly, how you can use it to change your life, your leadership, and your decision-making.

The limbic system: the emotional center

The Mind of a Leader

The limbic system is one of the oldest parts of your brain and evolved to survive. It is the cause of emotions, quick desires, and instinctive actions.

Its most common parts are:

Amygdala: Central for emotions such as fear, anger, and happiness.

Hippocampus: Responsible for memory and association with past experiences.

Hypothalamus: Controls your body's response to stress and emotions.

This system is designed to act quickly and put your safety first. For example, if you're walking down the street and see a shadow that looks like a predator's, your limbic system kicks in before you can process whether it's an animal or a moving branch.

The problem is that the system cannot distinguish between real and perceived threats. That's why you may get angry at innocuous comments or make hasty decisions when you're under stress.

The cerebral cortex: the voice of reason
The second corner of the ring is the cerebral cortex, specifically the prefrontal cortex, which houses the main functions: planning, thinking, reasoning, and self-control.

The crust does not react quickly. Analyze, analyze, and quantify best practices based on available data. It helps you:

Meditate before you speak.

Assess the risks and benefits.
Make appropriate and wise decisions.
However, it takes time. As the limbic system screams "Act now!", the cortex whispers "Wait a minute, let's figure this out." Have you ever wondered why it's so hard to stay calm when arguing or saying no to dessert while eating? This is war.

The limbic system tells you:

"Respond now and protect yourself." Eat that cake, you deserve it
Right now, your cerebral cortex is trying to say:

"If you scream, you will." to destroy the relationship."
"You don't want cake, remember your purpose."
When this struggle is stressful, the balance can shift to the limbic system. This is called psychological cheating and is one of the main reasons why many times we make the decisions that we then do, those controlled by the limbic system tend to:

Acting impulsively when there are conflicts.
Making decisions based on fear or pressure.
Loss of social trust due to emotional instability.
On the other hand, leaders who learn to balance both forces can:

Respond instead of reacting.
inspires confidence and tranquility.
Make smart decisions that benefit the team and the organization.
Good leadership doesn't mean ignoring ideas;

How to Win Your Inner War

The good news is that you don't have to be a slave to your thoughts or a rational robot. The key is to train your brain so that both systems work in harmony.

1. Be alert
Mindfulness strengthens the connection between the prefrontal cortex and the limbic system, allowing you to better manage your actions. Take a few minutes each day to analyze your thoughts and feelings without judging them.

2. Control Center
Severe stress can increase the reactions of the limbic system. Create an environment that promotes calm, such as regular breaks, relaxing music, and even a tidy workspace.

3. Learn self-control
When faced with an emotional crisis, try to take a deep breath before acting. Take a deep breath and give the bark time to intervene.

4. Consider your decisions
At the end of the day, weigh your decisions. Do you behave emotionally or intellectually? These exercises can help you recognize patterns and expand your knowledge.

Change your life and leadership immediately
Your brain has two best friends, but only one should guide you in every situation. Understanding and managing the battle between the limbic system and the cerebral cortex is not just a practical skill; That's the difference between living passively and leading with purpose.

Imagine what you could do if every decision you made was aligned with your goals and beliefs, and if you could address each problem appropriately and clearly. The future is not a dream, but a real possibility.

True leadership starts within you, where thoughts and feelings meet.

EMOTIONS AND THEIR ROLE IN DECISION-MAKING

Do you think that the most important decisions in your life are based on your imagination? Think again. Every step you take, every choice you make is deeply influenced by a quiet but powerful engine: your emotions.

For many years we have believed that common sense is the only reliable guide. We are told that emotions are distractions that we must ignore. But it's true and will forever change the way you look at decision-making: emotions are not the enemy. They inspire.

In this blog, we explore how emotions influence your decisions, why emotions are important to achieving your goals, and how you can use this knowledge to change your life and impact the world.

Why are emotions important?
Emotions are not simply reactions to the environment around us. They are an inner compass that guides you through uncertainty, a radar that detects opportunities and threats before you notice them.

Scientifically, emotions originate in the limbic system, the area of the brain responsible for processing emotional information and linking it to memories, past experiences, and future expectations. Not only does it help you survive, but it also helps you understand the world.

Surprising facts
Neuroscientist Antonio Damasio found that people with parts of the brain responsible for processing affected emotions have difficulty making decisions, even in simple tasks such as choosing between two identical foods. A healthy, emotionless mind is dead.

The role of emotions in decision-making
Help set priorities
Common sense alone is not enough in many decisions in modern life. Emotions help you determine what's important, analyze the information that affects you, and focus on what's really important.

Early warning systems are being developed
Fear protects you, anger drives you to action, and sadness controls your thinking. Every emotion has a purpose, and understanding it allows you to harness its power instead of controlling it.

Positive Action
Remember the last time you made a bold decision? You may do it out of curiosity, excitement, or even a little fear. Without feelings, nothing.

They connect people
In life, your decisions affect more than you. When you make decisions based on feelings like compassion and empathy, you have a positive impact on those around you.

The myth of pure reason
We live in an age that values logic and data. They teach us that being smart and being strong are the same thing. But this belief overlooks something important: we are not the rational machines we sometimes think, but emotional and thinking beings.

The secret is not in choosing emotions and thoughts, but in combining them. The reason is that the prefrontal cortex is closely related to the limbic system. Together they form an unbeatable team capable of making intelligent strategic decisions.

How to use your emotions
1. Understand your emotions
The first step to understanding your emotions is to understand them. Use tools like Plutchik's Wheel of Emotions to name your emotions and understand where they're coming from.

2. Think before you act
Pause for an important decision. Ask yourself: what emotions prompted you to make that decision? Is it fear,

joy, or despair? Understanding your emotions gives you the strength to overcome them.

3. Find the balance
Don't ignore your feelings, but don't let them control you. Use common sense to analyze facts and feelings to provide context and purpose for your choices.

4. Develops Emotional Intelligence
Emotional intelligence not only improves your relationships, but it's the key to effective decision-making. Learn to control your emotions and understand the emotions of others.

Leadership and Impact on Success
Leaders who ignore emotions lose touch with their teams. Conversely, a leader who understands his or her role creates a culture of trust, motivation, and loyalty. What kind of leader do you want to be?

Your emotions are not obstacles, they are tools to create a community capable of channeling and transforming reality. Understanding them will allow you to:

Make clear decisions.
Develop trust and empathy.
Manage chaos with clarity and humanity.
Change your relationship with your emotions today
Imagine: every decision you make in life is aligned with your values and goals. When emotions and thoughts work together, they don't conflict with each other. While this is possible, it is not a distant dream;

THE ROLE OF EMOTIONAL INTELLIGENCE IN LEADERSHIP

Over the years, we've been taught that good leaders are always right, show authority with numbers, impeccable methods, and misconceptions. But let me tell you something: great leaders are not only known for their IQ, but also for their emotional intelligence (EI).

This isn't just a trend or a buzzword, it's a scientifically backed fact. If you haven't focused on your emotional intelligence, you may be neglecting your most powerful tool for influencing, inspiring, and leaving a lasting impression on the people you lead.

Are you ready to challenge your leadership beliefs? Let's see how emotional intelligence changes everything.

What is emotional intelligence and why is it so important?
Emotional intelligence, a term popularized by Daniel Goleman, refers to the ability to better understand, manage, and use one's own and others' emotions.

In terms of leadership, it means more than being kind or compassionate. Dog:

Connect honestly with your team.
Better management of stress and anxiety.

The Mind of a Leader

You make rational and honest decisions.
Five Critical Components of Leadership Intelligence
Self-awareness: understanding your emotions and how your emotions influence decision-making.
Self-control: Practice your response to respond, not to act.

Medium Motivation: Having a clear vision and motivating others. Major English
Compassion: Understanding the feelings and perspectives of others.

Social Skills: Building strong relationships and resolving conflicts effectively.
Debunking common beliefs: "Leadership is subjective"
It's time to bust the biggest myths about leadership: facts and data are enough.

A leader may have a good strategy, but if they can't connect with their team, the strategy will fail. why? Because people don't follow cold charts or analysis. The emotions continue. They follow people who inspire them and make them feel important.

The Science Behind Emotions in Leadership
The limbic system is the emotional center of our brain and plays an important role in how we process information and make decisions. Research shows that emotions are the "glue" that connects people, builds trust, and creates engagement.

Leaders with high intelligence are able to ignite the inner strength of their teams and align their ideas with the organization's goals. It's not magic; This is neuroscience.

Page 68

The Incredible Leadership Benefits of Emotional Intelligence

Building sustainable teams
When you lead with emotional intelligence, you can help your team cope with change, overcome obstacles, and focus on goals, even in times of uncertainty.

Cultivate a culture of trust
Compassion and open communication make people feel valued, heard, and respected. This improves cooperation and reduces the number of employees.

Effective conflict resolution
A leader with EI is not afraid of conflict and approaches it wisely, understands the basic issues, and finds ways to strengthen relationships.

Workforce Development
Workers don't work for numbers; When they feel that their leaders understand their needs and care about their lives, productivity increases.

Call to Action: Elevating Your Leadership Through Awareness
Do you realize your powers? Emotional intelligence is not something sophisticated or "extra". It is the basis of good leadership in the 21st century

But here's the problem: EI doesn't happen overnight. This is the muscle you need to train. It's a journey toward self-knowledge, authentic connection, and emotional control.

Are you ready to take the first step?

The Mind of a Leader

Three actions to start today
Think: Take 10 minutes at the end of each day to see how you can take care of your thoughts and those of your team.

Active listening: I try to listen more than words. What kind of attitude do the people you lead display?
Learning and Development: Invest in personal and professional development. Books, seminars, conferences... All inclusive.
The future of leadership awaits
The world doesn't need many leaders who just give orders and do things. You need leaders who inspire, connect, and uplift others.

Do you want to be that leader? Then start by developing your emotional intelligence. Because the power you can have in your team, your community, and the world is the best thing you can do for yourself.

Don't wait for change to come to you. Be the change. Encourage. direct. Change that.

James Lass

HOW EMOTIONS INFLUENCE OUR CHOICES

Have you ever wondered why you sometimes make decisions that seem contradictory? Buy things you don't need, have a relationship that doesn't make you happy, or take a job that doesn't suit you. Spoiler alert: You're not anonymous. You're human. Like all of us, your decisions are made by a powerful ally (and sometimes enemy): your mind.

Do you want to know how this phenomenon works and, more importantly, how you can use it to make life-changing decisions? Welcome to this exciting world where science and logic come together to reveal secrets of your choice.

Challenge the belief: "I make decisions with my head, not with my heart"
Have you ever been told that decision-making should be fair and reasonable? This emotion is an obstacle that you must overcome. Well, it's time to dispel this myth.

Neuroscience shows that without emotions we cannot make decisions. Neuroscientist Antonio Damasio studied patients with damage to the areas of the brain responsible for emotional reactions. What's next? They can analyze data very well, but they can't decide between two seemingly simple options.

This means that our emotions are not limited to affect;

Limbic System: Your Emotional GPS

The Mind of a Leader

In your brain, the limbic system functions as a command center. Here, emotions such as fear, joy, sadness, and happiness are processed. These emotions create signals that your brain uses to evaluate the world around you and guide your choices.

Luck: When something makes you happy, you can choose it.
Fear: It prevents you from taking risks, even if the benefits are good.
Anger: It clouds your judgment and makes you make rash decisions.
The limbic system is very active. So much so that it can influence your decision before the prefrontal cortex (the logical part of your brain) has time to step in.

The power of emotions in everyday decisions
Consider this. Every decision you make, from what to eat to how to behave during important meetings, is filled with excitement. Even seemingly rational decisions, such as investing, have emotional expectations: Will they make you feel safe? Will it bring you closer to success?

Emotions are mental shortcuts. Without them, every decision would be long and exhausting. But here's the thing: sometimes these shortcuts can lead you down the wrong path.

The Science of Emotional Bias
While emotion is important, it can also cause us to make errors in judgment. Some examples:
Confirmation bias: looking for information that is consistent with how you already feel.
Overconfidence: Being confident can cause you to ignore important risks.

Fear of failure: It can discourage you and prevent you from making life-changing decisions.
But all is not lost. The key is not to ignore your emotions, but to learn to understand and control them.

How to Use Your Mind to Make Positive Choices
Pay attention to how you feel: Before making a decision, ask yourself: How am I feeling right now? Naming your thoughts can help explain how they affect you.

Look closely: Is the reaction temporary or does it indicate something deeper? If you're not calm, wait before making a decision.

Ask yourself "the future": Imagine how you would feel after making a decision. If the ideas are good and fit your values, it may be the right choice.

Integration of thoughts and feelings: It is not the elimination of thoughts, but the balance of thoughts and rational thought. Together they form a dynamic duo to make efficient decisions.

A surprising mindset for tough decisions
When you begin to understand and control your thoughts, something amazing happens:

You make decisions that are more aligned with your goals and beliefs.
You become an effective and compassionate leader.
You stop being on autopilot and start making smart decisions.
Your next step: regaining your decision-making power
You make hundreds or thousands of decisions every day. Some are small; Some people can change your life. The

The Mind of a Leader

question is: do you make decisions or do your thoughts make decisions for you?

Now that you know the important role the heart plays, it's time to take action. respiration. to meditate. Give each option the option it deserves.

Because the power to change your life isn't limited to choosing the "right" or the "wrong." It is a choice to feel with awareness, purpose, and courage.

Not far from your best type. This is a choice.

TECHNIQUES TO REGULATE EMOTIONS UNDER PRESSURE

The Master of Your Reactions

Have you ever felt like you were about to have a heart attack in a stressful situation? You lose control of your emotions, your hands tremble, your thoughts become dark, and your words seem to drown in a sea of anxiety.

Stress can bring out the good or the bad in us, and it's not the situation itself that makes the difference, but what we do. Here's the truth: The key to success in critical moments is not avoiding emotions, but learning to manage them for your own benefit.

Today we're going to debunk the myth that emotions interfere with decision-making under stress and show you how to turn emotions into very good tools. Be prepared, because these tips will not only change your career, but they will also change your life.

Challenge the belief: "Stress brings out the worst in us"
Most people believe that stress makes us think and feel bad. But this is just a myth. Stress doesn't define you; Stress won't define you. Why, why?

Neuroscience has discovered something surprising: when stressed, the brain activates two main systems:

The limbic system, which controls our emotional responses (such as fear or anger).
Preschooler, responsible for logical thinking and self-control.
When you're stressed, your limbic system takes over and you become agitated. But here's the kicker: Through exercise, you can strengthen your prefrontal cortex and regain control.
The Control of Emotional Regulation
Controlling emotions does not mean repressing them. It means getting to know them, understanding what they say, and responding, not ignoring them. It's like learning to surf without letting it take you.

If you possess these skills you will be able to:

Make clearer and more effective decisions, even when faced with problems.

Maintain professional health and personal relationships. Increase your resilience and reduce the impact of stress on your health. Chapter
Are you ready to get started? These are the techniques you need to manage your emotions when you're stressed.

1. Breathing: Your first line of defense
When stress increases, your breathing becomes faster and sends stress signals to your brain. Stop the cycle with this simple but powerful trick:

How to do it:
Deep in your nose for 4 seconds.
Hold your breath for 4 seconds.
Open your mouth slowly for 6-8 seconds.
Why it works: It activates your parasympathetic nervous system, which is responsible for calming you down. In a matter of minutes, you'll feel a new sense of clarity.

2. Emotion Etiquette: Name the Master
During stressful times, your emotions can feel like an uncontrollable whirlwind. This is where emotional cues come into play.

How to do it:
When you feel a strong emotion, say out loud (or silently): "This is _____ (fear, sadness, anxiety, etc.)".

Why it works: Research shows that emotional naming can help activate the prefrontal cortex to reduce stress. It's like turning on a light bulb in a dark room; Suddenly everything becomes more manageable.

3. Mental Rejuvenation: Change the Surface, Change the World

Page 76

Stress isn't bad; This may confuse us. Cognitive restructuring is changing the way we interpret a situation.

How to do it:
Ask:

What opportunities does this challenge offer me?
What is the worst that can happen? Chapter
Regardless of the outcome, what can I learn?
What it does: This exercise activates parts of the brain associated with positive thinking and reduces stress responses.

4. The Connection with the Body: Archiving in the Present
Under stress, the mind resorts to a tragic event, to repeat the mistakes of the past. Going back to this time you can do it from one place.

How to do it:
Try the "5-4-3-2-1" technique:

Find up to 5 things you can find.
Name 4 things you can touch.
Listen to three sounds around you.
Notes 2 Kisses the smell.
Take a deep breath 1 time.
Why it works: It keeps your mind in the moment and keeps you away from emotional stress.

5. Learn self-esteem: be their friend
If you make a mistake under pressure, it's easy to beat yourself up with negative thoughts. Instead, choose to love yourself.

How to do it:
Accept your thoughts: "This is hard, but I can do it."
Tell a friend, "It's okay to make mistakes"; It's important to learn from that."
Why it works: Self-love lowers cortisol (stress hormone) levels and increases resilience.

Conclusion: You can and will be ready to face anything
When you learn to control your emotions under pressure, it doesn't mean you can handle more problems. You will be someone who inspires confidence, leads calmly, makes clear and rational decisions.

Can you imagine the impact it would have on your personal life, career, and relationships?

Knowledge isn't the only thing in the box. This is a call to action. From today on, when you feel most stressed, stop, breathe and use these techniques. Put the stress on your partner and make them work for you, not you.

Because life is not about hiding from the storm, but about learning to weather it with courage and strength. Then you're good to go.

The power of hope in the eye of the hurricane
Have you ever felt anxiety when you're stressed? Do you wish you could stay calm when everything around you seems to be falling apart? Let me tell you something: the problem is not the stress itself, but how you deal with it.

In a world full of deadlines, expectations, and constant challenges, learning to control your emotions is not a luxury, but an essential skill. It's the difference between trusting leadership and being cautious, between moving toward a goal and feeling paralyzed.

Today I will talk about scientific techniques that will help you control your emotions in the most important moments and how you can turn stress into your strongest friend.

Let's guess the story: "Anxiety controls me"
Many people believe that anxiety is our enemy, a monster that can't control our lives. But the truth is; Stress is just a message from your brain. This is your internal alarm that tells you that something needs your attention.

The real problem is not anxiety, but how you look and how you act. You can let it consume you or learn how to guide it to make better decisions.

What happens to your brain when you're stressed?
When you're stressed, your brain goes into fight-or-flight mode. The limbic system, specifically the amygdala, sends alarm signals that trigger emotions such as fear, anxiety or depression. This helps to react quickly in real situations, but in today's world this process is often hyperactive.

The result? You lose the power of your prefrontal cortex, the part of the brain responsible for decision-making, planning, and creativity. It's like trying to drive a Ferrari with the handbrake on.

But don't worry: with the right ideas, you can regain control and turn your strong emotions into tools to move forward.

The Mind of a Leader

Energy Management for Stress Management in Stress

1. Breathe to regain control

Remember that breathing is one of the most powerful tools for calming the mind. Try this:

4-4-8 Breathing: Inhale for 4 seconds, hold for 4 seconds, exhale slowly for 8 seconds.
This activates your parasympathetic system, called the stress brake, to help you recover.

2. Practice happiness

Choose an image, memory, or expression that brings you peace and confidence. When you feel anxious, close your eyes and bring that image to your mind. This is a way to remind your brain that stress doesn't last forever and that you've faced problems before.

3. Redirect your thinking through cognitive restructuring

Cognitive restructuring will change the way you interpret a situation.

Instead of thinking, "This is a mess and I can't do it." emotional response.

4. Use positive images

Close your eyes and imagine the best possible outcome of the situation you are facing. Look at everything in detail: how you think, how you act, how you achieve your goals. Not only does this make you feel good, but it also trains your brain to find solutions instead of focusing on problems.

5. Connecting with your body

Stress causes physical stress. Practice techniques such as body awareness or mindful stretching to release energy. For example, pay attention to your shoulders, jaw, or

Page 80

hands: are they tense? Make an effort to make them easier.

Secrets of resilient leaders

Great leaders are not immune to stress. The difference is that they know how to control it. They develop their skills to stay calm, think clearly, and make the right decisions even in the most difficult situations.

Did you know that some of the most successful leaders, from Olympians to CEOs of large companies, use these strategies? Research backs up its benefits, and you can benefit from them, too.

Why controlling your behavior under stress can change your life.

When you learn to control your behavior:

You'll make better decisions: No more distractions you'll regret later.
You will strengthen your relationships: You will be able to communicate openly and willingly even in difficult times.
Your self-confidence will increase: Knowing that you can control every situation will give you unique power.
You will be a role model: Your actions will inspire others to find peace in the midst of chaos.
You're doing it now
Stress and pressure don't go away. But that's not a bad thing. What matters is how you choose to get to know them. Will you be the controller of your thoughts, or will you be the master of your thoughts?

The Mind of a Leader

Change starts here and now. Practice these skills. Apply them to your daily life. Because when you control your thoughts, you not only change your life, but you also inspire others to do the same.

Remember: Peace is not the absence of violence, but your ability to control violence.

Are you ready to take control and become the best version of yourself? Now is the time!

James Lass

NEUROPLASTICITY: HOW TO TRANSFORM YOUR MIND TO LEAD BETTER

Have you ever felt that your leadership skills are limited due to your personality, education, or even age? Do you think that great leaders are born, not made? It's time to bust this myth!

Science proves that your brain can change and change throughout your life. This remarkable ability is called neuroplasticity, and what it reveals is nothing less than a shift in the way we understand leadership. Yes, you can train your brain to be an effective, inspiring, and down-to-earth leader. No matter what stage of your career you are at or how you feel now, your mind is moving and now is the time to harness your power to transform your leadership.

The brain: a machine for change
For many years, the brain was seen as a fixed structure that started early in life and then became fixed, unable to change. But neuroscience overturns this belief. Your brain is like a muscle: the more you train it, the stronger and faster it becomes.

Neuroplasticity is the brain's ability to reorganize itself and create new neural connections based on experience, learning, and even environmental changes. This means you can change your brain to improve other skills, such as leadership.

What does that mean for you as a leader?
You can change your mind. If you've ever thought you were too "impulsive" or "too popular" to be a good leader, neuroplasticity offers a way out. You can train your brain to make calmer decisions, be more compassionate, and improve your resilience in the face of adversity.

You will be able to learn how to deal with stress and anxiety. Leaders often face serious challenges. The good news is that the brain can learn to control the emotions that arise during stressful situations. By training your brain, you can learn to stay calm, make better decisions, and be a positive role model for your team.

You can encourage creativity and innovation. Today, technology is the key to success. If you ever felt like you weren't a "creative person," neuroplasticity teaches you that we all have the ability to innovate. You just need to exercise and feed the areas of your brain that are responsible for creating things.

You can improve your communication skills. Great leaders know how to communicate well. Neuroscience shows that practicing communication skills improves neural connections with empathy and trust, important skills for any leader.
The Power of Reshaping Your Mind: 4 Ways to Help Leadership

1. Cognitive Repetition: The Secret of Mastery

Neuroplasticity is primarily activated through repetition. The more you practice, the more neural connections develop and the skill becomes easier. As a leader, you can use this to develop creative new solutions or develop your own intellectual skills. For example, practicing quick decision-making in stressful situations strengthens the part of the brain that needs to react quickly and efficiently.

2. Meditation and Meditation: The Power of Imagination
Daily meditation or meditation practice has been scientifically proven to increase the brain's ability to adapt to change. Not only does this improve your mental health, but it also increases activity in areas of the brain related to empathy, decision-making, and emotional regulation. As a leader, training your mind to stay in the present moment without getting caught up in stress or frustration will allow you to make wiser decisions and be a beacon of calm for your team.

3. Continuous learning: the key to evolution
Neuroplasticity is also closely related to continuous learning. Every time you learn something new, your brain creates new connections. Leaders who never stop learning, keep up with the latest industry trends, best practices, and new leadership tools, strengthen their mindset, and are able to adapt and change. Don't stop growing.

4. Emotional and psychological challenges: drivers of change
Stepping out of your comfort zone is one of the best ways to promote neuroplasticity. Facing new challenges, overcoming difficult obstacles, and learning how to deal with conflict effectively awakens parts of your brain that

you didn't know you had. Great leaders do not shy away from challenges;

The Surprising Benefits of Bringing Neuroplasticity to Leadership

What most people don't understand is that neuroplasticity not only improves learning, but can also change the way you see the world. As a leader, it makes you flexible, flexible, and most importantly, understanding of your team's needs.

Better decision-making: Training your brain to think better under pressure increases your ability to make better decisions.

Reduce stress: When you learn to control your emotions and see challenges as opportunities for growth, stress becomes a friend, not an enemy.

Have deep empathy and connection with your teams: Neuroplastic leaders know how to connect with their teams, understand their needs, and respond with empathy.

Nature and innovation: A brain trained to think outside the box has the ability to find new solutions and adapt quickly to change.

It's time to change your leadership!
The future of leadership is not predetermined, it is in your hands. Your mind has the ability to change and adapt to the challenges of the 21st century. Neuroplasticity is the key to unlocking a leader's full potential.

Don't settle for being an average leader. Be the leader who inspires, who creates, who transforms! The world needs leaders who understand that change starts in the mind. Are you ready to change yours?

WHAT IS NEUROPLASTICITY AND WHY DOES IT MATTER?

Imagine if you could redesign your brain to become smarter, stronger, more creative, and able to achieve goals you never imagined possible. Does this sound like science fiction to you? But that's not the case. This is the promise of neuroplasticity, and the best part: it's totally true!

Neuroplasticity is the brain's amazing power to reorganize, adapt, and make new connections throughout life. We are no longer tied to the fixed structures that we believe define our spiritual destiny. You can change your thoughts and, therefore, your life.

If you've ever believed that your abilities were predetermined, that your personality or intelligence was fixed, it's time to break these myths. Neuroplasticity defies everything you thought you knew about the brain. This concept of transformation tells us that you can adjust your mindset to become the best version of yourself.

The Neuroplasticity Revolution: Change Your Brain, Change Your Life
Neuroplasticity tells us a clear fact: our brains are not a fixed structure, but are constantly changing, even at the end of our lives. This doesn't just happen when we're children, the adult brain has the ability to reset and grow every time we learn something new or face a challenging experience.

But here's the surprise: you can use neuroplasticity to actively shape the person you want to be! Would you like to be more resilient in difficult times, more creative when faced with difficult challenges, or more empathetic and connected to others? Neuroplasticity makes it possible. Just as your muscles get stronger when you exercise, your brain responds as you practice and learn.

Why is neuroplasticity the key to effective leadership?
We live in a world that is changing faster than ever. Adaptability is the difference between success and failure. In this case, leaders who understand and leverage neuroplasticity are one step ahead. for? Because they know that change is not only possible, but also desirable and necessary.

Imagine being a leader who doesn't handle pressure easily, but at the same time inspires your team to innovate, think outside the box, and achieve extraordinary results. You can achieve this when you train your mind to be flexible and strong.

It's not just a pun Neuroplasticity activates parts of the brain for creativity, effective decision-making, and problem-solving. Leaders who understand and apply this can make decisions faster, build deeper relationships with their teams, and most importantly, lead with vision and purpose.

The Amazing Benefits of Neuroplasticity
Neuroplasticity not only gives you cognitive advantages, but it also affects deeper aspects of your life, such as your mood, relationships, and health. Here are some surprising benefits of this scientific marvel:

Better emotional resilience.
Instead of reacting to difficult situations with panic or despair, you can train your mind to stay calm and think clearly in the midst of chaos. Leaders who use these skills are more effective in times of uncertainty.

Added skills.
Neuroplasticity allows you to create new neural connections, which means being able to find new solutions to problems. If you've ever felt like creativity wasn't your thing, it's time to change that belief.

Improved decision-making.
A rational mind can effectively evaluate options and make better, faster decisions. No more confusing decisions. Training your mind will allow you to assess risk more accurately.

Strengthen relationships between people.
Neuroplasticity can boost your emotional intelligence. By activating the areas of your brain associated with empathy, you'll be able to connect with others, build stronger teams, and become a truly inspiring leader.
Reduce stress and tension.
A trained mind can learn to control emotions and reduce the negative effects of stress. Neuroplasticity can change your relationship with stress, helping you stay calm and clear even in the most difficult of times.

How to Start Neuroplasticity Today
Best of all, you don't have to be a genius or spend years studying to unlock neuroplasticity in your life. With consistent practice, you can make your mind more active, compassionate, and strong. Below are some key steps to start harnessing this power:

Exercise your mind.
Like any muscle, your mind needs exercise. Learning new things, solving puzzles, reading challenging books, or practicing new skills are all great ways to unlock neuroplasticity.

Meditation and Awareness.
These exercises strengthen neural connections related to the regulation of emotions and attention. They can help you be better prepared and make more informed decisions.

Break your habit.
Do something you wouldn't normally do: Try a new way to solve a problem or change the way you usually do it. This forces your thinking to change and make new connections.

Learn from failure.
Failure is an opportunity to change the way you think. When faced with a challenge, instead of getting discouraged, think about the new neural connections you can make from the experience.

Surround yourself with people who will propel you forward.
Improving relationships and encouraging healthy arguments and disagreements is a great way to create the psychological zone associated with empathy, creativity, and problem-solving.

BRAIN TRAINING TO DEVELOP NEW SKILLS

Break the Limits of Your Mind and Unleash Your Potential!

What if I told you that you have the ability to rewire your brain to learn any skill, no matter how difficult it is? Do you dare to believe that you can learn new skills, improve your performance, and push the limits of what you thought possible?

It's time to challenge limiting beliefs!

The human brain is more powerful than you think. With brain training, you will not only develop new skills, but you will also revolutionize your life. Whether you want to learn a new language, learn an instrument, improve your leadership skills, or even take your creativity to unimaginable levels, your brain has the ability to adapt, change, and evolve. The main thing is to learn how to use this power.

Today I'm going to show you how brain training can be the secret tool for unlocking skills you never thought you could develop. Best of all: you can get started now!

The Power of Neuroplasticity: The Secret to Changing Your Mind
Did you know that your brain is not a fixed object, but a dynamic organ that is constantly changing? This phenomenon is called neuroplasticity and allows the brain to learn, grow, and acquire new skills.
For many years it was thought that as we age, our brain stops developing. But this is a myth! Neuroplasticity suggests that we can continue to develop new

connections and skills throughout our lives. Every time you learn something new, your brain reorganizes itself and creates new neural pathways, creating skills that previously seemed impossible to achieve.

For example, do you want to improve your ability to make quick decisions under pressure? Your brain is capable of doing this, but it needs training. Are you looking to develop your creative or entrepreneurial skills? It's absolutely possible! The secret is how to challenge and train your brain to change and grow.

How does brain exercise work?
Brain training isn't magic. This is pure science. Just as we train our muscles to grow and strengthen, training our brain involves habits, repetitions, and stimulating activities to change and learn the brain. But it's not just about learning something: it's about learning how to maximize profits.

Below are some ways brain training can help you develop new skills:

1. Challenge your brain with new experiences.
The key to brain growth is to get out of your comfort zone. If you keep doing the same thing, your brain will eventually follow the same pattern. But when you're faced with a new challenge, like learning something new or solving a complex problem, you activate parts of your brain that weren't used before. It creates new neural connections that improve your ability to learn and adapt.

For example, if you decide to learn to play an instrument, your brain develops new neural pathways to coordinate your hands, play music, and understand sounds and notes. Although it may seem difficult at first, with regular practice the bonds will strengthen and your skills will improve quickly.

2. Deliberate action: it is not enough to do it, it must be done regularly.
Discussion is one of the most effective ways to develop new skills. It focuses on certain areas that need improvement and invests time and effort in improving them. If you do something without careful observation, you won't achieve much success. But if you move with clear intention and constant feedback, your brain will adapt quickly as you engage in the learning process.

3. Repetition: Exercise your brain through repetition.
The brain requires constant repetition to strengthen new neural connections. It's like when you work out at the gym: your muscles are weak at first, but over time and reps they get stronger. The same goes for cognitive skills such as decision-making, problem-solving, or language learning.

Every time you practice a skill, such as a new language or an artistic skill, your brain strengthens the connections associated with that process. The more you repeat this, the easier it will be for you to act or make decisions without thinking too much. Over time, new skills become second nature.

4. Visualization: train your mind for success.
Visualization is a powerful technique used by athletes and high-performance professionals to improve their skills. By designing a new skill in your brain, you activate the part of your brain that you use to perform it.

This allows your brain to function better in the real world.

For example, a leader who visualizes each step of a successful presentation can train their brain to improve communication skills, reduce nervousness, and boost self-confidence. Visualization is a mental exercise that accelerates the learning process and brings you closer to understanding.

Amazing Benefits of Brain Training
It's not just about learning new skills. Brain training has the following benefits:

Increased concentration and efficiency. By training your brain to focus on a specific task, you can improve your ability to concentrate and therefore be more productive.

Initialize memory. Regular mental exercises help strengthen short- and long-term memory and allow you to remember important information quickly and effectively.

Reduce stress and anxiety. Practices like meditation and mindfulness can train your brain to regulate your emotions and make it easier for you to manage stress.

Development of creativity. By challenging your brain to think in new ways, you open the door to endless creativity, allowing you to approach problems and challenges from a new perspective.

The Mind of a Leader

Page 96

THE GROWTH MINDSET APPLIED TO LEADERSHIP.

Transform Your Potential and Your Team's Potential

Have you ever wondered what separates great leaders from mediocre ones? What do people who are always one step ahead, adapt quickly to change, overcome obstacles, and lead their teams to success have in common? The answer lies in a simple but powerful mindset: growth.

If you still think that talent and leadership are natural qualities, it's time to reconsider that belief. The science behind a growth mindset shows that true leadership is not based on specific skills, but on the belief that you can always learn, adapt, and change. This attitude changes everything you know about what it means to be a leader.

What does growth prospect mean?

The term growth mindset was popularized by psychologist Carol Dweck. It showed that people who believe that their skills and abilities can be developed through effort, perseverance, and learning are more successful than those who believe that their talents are fixed and unchanging.

Growth-minded leaders understand that failure is not the end, but an opportunity to learn and grow. This attitude encourages them to see every challenge as a step towards success and not as an insurmountable obstacle. And the best part: you can apply these ideas at any time in your life.

The Mind of a Leader

In the context of leadership, a growth mindset means believing that as a leader, there is always something new to learn, there is always a way to improve your strategy, communication, influence, and ability to motivate a team. And that's the first step to real change!

Why is a growth mindset important for successful leadership?

1. Growth-oriented leaders are more adaptable

In a world that changes at the speed of light, the ability to adapt quickly is the key to success. Traditional leaders who have a fixed mindset see change as a threat. Growth-oriented leaders, on the other hand, see this as an opportunity.

When a leader has a growth mindset, they are motivated by challenges, not intimidation. This allows them to lead with agility, manage crises effectively, and seize new opportunities before everyone else. Rather than resisting innovation, they embrace change as a way to improve themselves and their teams.

This kind of thinking makes good leaders great leaders. Those who understand that learning never ends and that there is always room to grow become role models for their team. No matter how many years you've been leading, there will always be something new to learn that will take you to the next level.

2. Growth mindset drives resilience

Resilience is one of the most important qualities of a good leader. Leaders with a fixed mindset often take failure personally: "I'm not good at this" or "I wasn't born to do this," but leaders with a growth mindset see failure

Page 98

as a lesson. They know that every fall is an opportunity to wake up strong.

Strong leaders don't give up in difficult situations. Instead of giving up or being afraid of failure, look for ways to improve. Resilience is what allows great leaders to stay calm under pressure and lead their teams to effective solutions.

The world is full of uncertainty. Leaders who adopt a growth mindset will thrive in difficult times because they see problems as opportunities to learn and grow.

3. Growth-minded leaders motivate their teams to grow
Growth-minded leaders not only care about their own growth, but they also motivate their teams to do the same. True leadership is not about being the best, but about encouraging others and building a culture of growth within the team.

When a leader cultivates an environment where continuous learning is a given, team members feel empowered to take on new challenges and develop their skills. Not only does this increase productivity and performance, but it also strengthens employee loyalty and satisfaction.

In addition, leaders with a growth mindset encourage collaboration and teamwork, understanding that shared learning creates a culture of mutual support and growth.

4. The growth mindset drives innovation
Innovation is an important quality of any leader who wants to not only survive but also thrive. Strong-minded leaders tend to stick to traditional methods and fear risk.

The Mind of a Leader

In contrast, growth-minded leaders are constantly looking for new ways of doing things.

Creativity is not only thinking of new ideas, but also the willingness to fail and learn from those failures. With a growth mindset, leaders have the ability to make changes, test new strategies, and find innovative solutions to more complex problems.

How to implement a growth mindset in your leadership?
Here are some practical steps to start adopting a growth mindset in your leadership style:

1. Embrace challenges
A growth mindset is driven by challenges. Do not seek comfort; Look for opportunities to grow. Take on the most difficult projects and be an example of perseverance for your team.

2. Learn from failure
Failure is not the enemy. He is a teacher. When things don't go your way, instead of giving up or punishing yourself, ask yourself: What can I learn from this? What parts of the process can I improve?

3. Encourage continuous learning
Invest in yourself and your team. Learn new skills, update them, and always look for opportunities to expand your knowledge and skills. Remember that learning never ends.

4. Promote progress, not perfection
Progress, not perfection, is the hallmark of leadership and vision. Celebrate every breakthrough, every achievement,

no matter how small. This process provides the motivation and energy needed to continue growing.

5. *Cultivate a culture of growth*
As a leader, you have the ability to instill a culture of growth in your team. It encourages continuous learning, collaboration, and creativity. Embrace failure as part of the creative process and encourage everyone to continually learn and improve.

It's time to change your leadership
A growth mindset is more than a strategy; It is a way of life and training. Great leaders are not born with a gift, but they are capable of growing, learning, and improving every day.

It's time to let go of the beliefs that are holding you back from reaching your potential. A growth mindset is the path to becoming an effective, smart, and resilient leader.

If you want to be the leader you've always wanted to be —someone who inspires your team to reach new heights, faces challenges boldly, and always seeks change—then take action now. Do it now! Don't stop for anything. The future of leadership is in your hands!

DECISION-MAKING IN UNCERTAINTY SCENARIOS

The Power to Decide with Confidence in Chaos

Picture this: you are facing a critical juncture; A moment when every decision has the power to change the future, but you don't have all the information. You don't have all the answers. The future looks complicated, the danger is uncertain and the road ahead is cloudy. You feel trapped by the fear of failure and the pressure to act quickly.

What would you do in this situation?

If you're like most people, you're probably paralyzed. Uncertainty is dangerous. But here's the challenge: good leaders and professionals don't let themselves be paralyzed by uncertainty. Instead, they control it, understand it, and use it to their advantage. Making decisions under conditions of uncertainty is not only a challenge but also a skill that can be mastered.

You can do it too.

It's time to put aside the fear of uncertainty and turn to your heart to act with confidence. Making decisions in the dark is an art and you can master it!

The concept of security and truth

Page 102

We live in a world that values truth. Everywhere we are told that "everything must be under control" and that detailed planning and forecasting are the key to success. So what happens when life doesn't follow the perfect script?

What is true is what is unknown, what is not true. We live in a changing environment where markets change, trends evolve, resources become scarce and unpredictable conditions arise. This uncertainty can give us security, but it can also be the most important and transformative decision.

We can't control everything, but we can control our emotions towards the unknown.

The most successful leaders in the business and personal world aren't always the ones with the most knowledge or the right answers. Even if they don't have all the answers, they act confidently and manage risk effectively.

The research behind decision-making under uncertainty

The study of decision-making under uncertainty is based on two principles: information transfer and high risk. Both concepts are supported by neuroscience and cognitive psychology and are important for good decision-making in the mind.

1. Adaptive cognition: the ability to think beyond the predictable

Adaptive cognition is the brain's ability to adapt to new information and change quickly when the environment demands it. In situations of uncertainty, our brain is confronted with incomplete information, but it also looks for patterns and makes predictions based on what it knows, even if it is not enough.

Faithful leaders can make quick and effective decisions even if they can't see the outcome with certainty. Instead of being paralyzed, they do the best they can with the information they have and adjust course as conditions change. This flexibility allows good leaders to thrive in an environment of uncertainty.

Risk tolerance: the ability to accept the unknown
Fear of risk prevents many people from acting in the face of uncertainty. Risk can paralyze us or cause us to make bad decisions, but the important thing is to understand that risk is part of success. The important thing is not to eliminate the risk, but to manage it effectively.

Risk tolerance does not mean being at fault; It means being willing to move into the unknown, knowing that even if we don't have a clear map of the future, we have the tools to walk in the dark. A high-risk leader doesn't make hasty decisions, but they also don't let the fear of uncertainty consume them. Realize that every decision, even the one that seems risky, is an opportunity to learn and improve.

How to make the right decisions in times of uncertainty?
1. Accept uncertainty as a friend
Uncertainty is not your enemy, it is your best friend. When you know that full control is a surprise, you can let go of the pressure of having all the answers. Accepting the unknown gives you the freedom to make decisions without fear of failure. This is the first step to moving forward with confidence.

Page 104

Important question: What will I accomplish if I accept this uncertainty and use it to make decisions?

2. Develop the ability to make quick decisions and constantly adapt

In times of uncertainty, analysis paralysis can be your worst enemy. The best decision is not the best decision, but a quick decision allows you to move forward and make adjustments. Don't wait for all the information, use the available information to make the best decision and course correct if necessary.

Important Question: What is the worst thing that could happen to me if I decide now?

3. Prioritize action over perfection

Perfection is the enemy of success, especially when time is limited. Instead of looking for the best solution, focus on doing something and move on. It turns out that quick and bad decisions are often more effective than uncertain ones.

Original question: What can I do now to get closer to the solution, even if it is not perfect?

4. Trust your intuition and knowledge

Understanding is most useful when we encounter uncertainty. As a leader, you bring with you a lot of knowledge and experience, and your ability to use your imagination can be important in making good decisions in uncertain situations.

Important question: What is my gut telling me right now, based on my experience?

5. Learn from every decision

Remember, in times of uncertainty, there is no such thing as a "wrong" decision; Every decision is a learning process. If the results aren't what you wanted, analyze what happened, adjust your approach, and move on. True wisdom comes from experience, not perfection.

Important question: What can I learn from this outcome, whether it was successful or not?

Working time now

The uncertainty has not disappeared. We live in an uncertain and unpredictable world, and the ability to make confident decisions is one of the most important willpower skills. The future doesn't wait, and if you wait for uncertainty to disappear before making a decision, you're missing out on an important opportunity.

Today is control day. Be brave. Use uncertainty as a way to grow, learn, and progress. Every decision you make today brings you closer to the person you can become tomorrow.

Do it now! Uncertainty is fertile ground where great leaders sow their profits. It's time to plant your own.

James Lass

HOW THE BRAIN PROCESSES RISK AND AMBIGUITY

Master the Art of Making Bold Decisions

Picture this: you're facing a major decision that could change your life or career. There are two paths before you, but the problem is that you can't see the future. Both methods are uncertain and risky. The consequences of making mistakes are severe, but the crippling fear and indecision can be even more devastating. What are you doing?

Do you want to stop? Are you allowing yourself to get stuck in analysis paralysis, hoping to have all the answers before you do? Or do you have the courage to step up and make a bold decision, even if you're not sure who it is?

If you've encountered this problem before, you know that uncertainty and risks can arise. But no one tells you the truth that risk and uncertainty are inevitable. But most importantly, even if you don't have all the answers, you can train your brain to make better, faster decisions.

This is the power that great leaders and decision-makers understand. They will not wait for things to be clear before acting. They train themselves to check reality and make decisions without fear of failure. You can too.

Why are we afraid of risk and uncertainty?
To understand how the brain works is risky and confusing, we must first break down the assumptions of

these concepts. The human brain is designed to protect us and the feeling of uncertainty activates one of the most important parts of the brain, the amygdala. This structure is part of the limbic system and plays a role in our response to emotions, especially fear.

The amygdala raises the alarm when we are faced with danger or an uncertain decision. The brain warns us of real or perceived threats. That's why, when the future is uncertain, our strategy is to avoid taking risks, opt for safety and stay in our comfort zone. This protective instinct evolved to help us survive in a dangerous world, but in today's society this instinct can become a brake when we need a quick and bold decision.

What happens in our brain when we decide to take risks? Not only does the brain produce fear in response to risk, but it also uses many areas to calculate, analyze, and decide what to do. The two main areas are:

1. Prefrontal Cortex: Center for Decision Making and Decision Making
Faced with a dangerous decision, the prefrontal cortex (the newest, the brain of most of us) comes into play. This is the basis of our thinking, where we evaluate the rewards and consequences of each choice. This is where opinion is consulted and where we find information to make decisions.

But here's the thing: When the prefrontal cortex is responsible for making value decisions, it's in constant competition with the amygdala, which makes impulsive fear-based decisions. The balance between the two parts of the brain will determine whether we make good decisions or allow ourselves to succumb to fear.

2. Nucleus Accumbens: The Seat of Reward and Motivation

The nucleus Accumbens plays an important role in our persistence. This part of the brain is associated with the feeling of reward and is an area that is activated when we think about results, such as the joy or satisfaction of achieving a goal.

Risk isn't always bad. In fact, the human brain is designed to be reward-motivated even when there is uncertainty. If we can perceive risk over time, the accumulator core can create a sense of motivation that drives us to act in uncertain situations.

How do you make informed decisions in a world full of risks and complexity?

So how do you train your brain to better deal with risk and uncertainty? Here are some neuroscience tips you can use today to make better decisions:

1. Identify and manage fear

Fear is the brain's response to uncertainty, but it doesn't have to control you. The important thing is to identify when fear is blocking decision-making and open it up to effective action. Take a deep breath and stop. Decisions made under stress are often made during times of emotional stress. The amygdala can be powerful, but you have the power to calm it. Practice self-assessment to see what types of behaviors guide your decisions. This emotional awareness will allow you to control and focus on your fears.

2. Change the way you think about risk

Great leaders don't see risk as something to be avoided, they see it as an opportunity. Replace fear with curiosity.

"What if I can't?" Ask yourself, "What if this works?" Start asking. All risks are valuable, and you can unlock mental rewards by considering the consequences of making bold decisions. Reframe your thinking to see risk as an investment in your growth.

3. Make decisions based on data, not emotions
When fear and emotions play a role in decision-making, data and emotions also play a role. Use your prefrontal cortex to your advantage. Instead of relying solely on yourself, try to analyze the available information and make an informed decision. Good leaders don't worry about uncertainty, but instead engage in smart plans and changes.

4. Accept uncertainty as part of the process
This is where the real magic happens. Uncertainty is not a barrier; It is the raw material of growth and innovation. Instead of trying to escape confusion, use confusion as an opportunity to learn and grow. Don't look for absolute values; Look for small, measurable metrics that you can adjust over time.

5. Build mental resilience
Making decisions in conditions of danger and ambiguity is not easy, but mental stability allows you to recover quickly from failure and adapt to new situations. Resilience is a skill that is learned. Develop your ability to manage stress with a positive, solution-oriented approach.

Now is the time to act!
The dangers and complications never end, but you can train your brain to deal with them with confidence, clarity, and effectiveness. The future is uncertain and

that's where great leaders can thrive. Risk and complexity are your allies, not your enemies.

It's time to stop waiting for the "right time." Perfection does not exist. The real magic is in the action, in having the courage to make decisions even when you don't have all the answers.

Your brain is prepared for it. This is your time too.

NEUROLOGICAL STRATEGIES FOR DECIDING IN CRITICAL SITUATIONS

The Science of Action Under Pressure

Have you ever faced a situation where your future depends on a decision you need to make right away? Maybe it's a business opportunity you can't pass up or a personal issue that forces you to take action. At that point, the pressure may be so high that it is easy to interfere with the examination of the organs. We hesitate, hoping that the perfect answer will magically appear.

But let me tell you something for sure: you don't need a perfect answer. What you need is the ability to make quick and effective decisions, even if you don't have all the information. Yes, they can be trained.

The Science of Decision-Making Under Pressure

The human brain is designed to make decisions. However, when faced with a serious problem, our brain's decision-making processes collide. On the one hand, we have the prefrontal cortex, which is responsible for making logical and logical decisions, and on the other hand, we have the amygdala, which instinctively responds to fear and panic.

The prefrontal cortex is the center of our conscious, controlled mind, where we weigh right and wrong, plan strategies, and calculate long-term consequences. However, during times of high stress, the amygdala becomes active, triggering the "fight or flight" response, which can lead to anxiety and make it difficult to make rational decisions.

The conflict between fear and reason is the biggest problem when we are faced with difficult decisions. The key is to overcome fear, but manage it so that it doesn't interfere with our ability to act. This is where brain techniques come into play: you can train your brain to make decisions quickly and clearly, even in difficult situations.

Neurological mechanisms for making smart decisions under stress

1. Recognize and change emotional responses

The first step to making effective decisions in difficult situations is to recognize the effects of stress on the brain.

When you experience stress, your brain reacts emotionally. Fear is natural, but you shouldn't let it control you. Senior leaders and decision-makers are good at distinguishing between emotion and rational response.

When you feel your depression, stop and breathe. Deep breathing activates the vagus nerve, which reduces responses to nerve impulses and helps reduce activation of the amygdala. This simple action allows you to back off and regain control. By doing this, you create a hub of activity in your prefrontal cortex so that you can think clearly.

2. Make decisions based on facts, not hypotheses
The brain tends to look for patterns and facts, especially when faced with uncertainty. However, absolute certainty is rarely found, so we must train our minds to make decisions based on what we have rather than what we want to have.

Great leaders train their brains to think that making quick decisions is more important than waiting for all the pieces to fall into place. In some cases, taking action quickly yields more results, allowing you to adjust your course accordingly.

To do this, stop your thoughts and focus on what is in front of you. Ask important questions, quickly analyze the results, and take action. Over time, this will improve your ability to make quick decisions, even in the face of uncertainty.

3. Use the power of visualization to reshape your mind
One of the most powerful tools in a difficult situation is visualization. Top athletes use this technique to prepare

their brains for challenges. By thinking about how to respond well to difficult situations, you can train your brain to respond well when the time is right.

Visualization is effective because it activates the same areas of the brain that are activated during action. By imagining yourself making quick and efficient decisions, you rewire your brain to act with confidence. Not only will this boost your confidence, but it will also reduce the stress you often experience when making difficult decisions.

4. Make small decisions to act fast
When you're faced with a big problem, you might feel compelled to make a big decision that will change everything. But that is not the case. The best decisions in the most difficult situations aren't big or terrible. The key is to make small, measurable progress.

The human brain is designed to move forward, and a small step toward a solution can have a bigger impact than waiting for everything to be perfect. Plus, every little thought gives you more information, allowing you to change and improve your focus without getting paralyzed.

5. Trust your experiences and instincts
Neuroscience shows us that the human brain has incredible memory systems and the ability to use past experiences to make quick decisions. This system is controlled by a process called decision-making, in which your brain uses unconsciously stored information to take action without much analysis.

So believe in what you've experienced. If you've been in a similar situation before, your brain already has a "fingerprint" of how to react. In most cases, the best decision for a problem is the one that is made intuitively based on your knowledge and experience. When your gut tells you something, don't ignore it.

Act Now
It's true: the most powerful decisions aren't always the right ones, but ones that are made confidently and quickly. In critical situations, time is of the essence. The most successful leaders are those who act when others walk away.

Now it's time to take control. If you train your brain to handle stress, make small, honest decisions, and trust your gut and intuition, you'll not only improve your decision-making ability, but you'll also become a more confident and courageous leader.

The risk of doing nothing is greater than the risk of making a mistake. So act now, because the future does not wait. Your mind is primed to make confident decisions even in the most important moments. It's time for you to shine.

THE IMPORTANCE OF CONFIDENCE IN INFORMED INTUITION

Why Should You Trust Your Instinct to Make Decisions?

Have you ever faced a difficult decision and even though you didn't have all the information, you always knew what to do? That undeniable feeling that even if you're not sure, you've chosen the right path. In business culture, as in everyday life, the power of the mind is often irrelevant. We learn that smart decisions are based on hard data, rigorous analysis, and systematic planning. But the science of the human brain and the experiences of successful leaders prove otherwise: intuition, when properly nurtured and informed, is one of our most powerful tools.

Today I want you to take a step towards the truth of change: Seeing is not an accident or a strange feeling. It is the result of a trained brain and mental processes that are closely related to knowledge and experience. And most importantly: you can learn to trust him.

What is insight and why is it important? First, let's define what we mean by the concept of intelligence. It is the ability to make quick and rational decisions based not only on personal data, but also on accumulated knowledge, past experiences, and simple signals that our brain collects. It's like having a special psychic power that mixes what you know with what you feel.

Page 116

Imagine you're in a meeting room and you hear different requests. You don't have all the numbers, you don't know all the background, but something inside tells you that this idea is good. He's amazing at work. It's the perfect balance between logic and emotion, between hard facts and real experience.

But this is surprising: intuition is not magic. It is the ability to access more information stored in the brain, which processes it faster than we know. In fact, when you make a quick decision, your brain creates thousands of ideas that can't always be explained logically, but are completely logical and based on the previous situation.

The Science of Perception: Your Brain Is Always Learning
The human brain is very useful for pattern recognition. Even without realizing it, your brain is constantly collecting information. As you interact with the world, whether it's at work, in relationships, or even in your personal life, you create a complex web of experiences that your brain stores and uses to make predictions.

Did you know that every time you make a decision, your brain sifts through a huge library of past information, even if you don't know it? This network of knowledge has your "instincts".

This process is called active learning. Neuroscience has shown that the brain can recognize patterns and make decisions without our knowledge. Whenever we make a decision in a complex environment, our brain combines what we already know with the new situation, giving us a better and faster solution. This is mental power: the brain is trained to work quickly and efficiently.

The Mind of a Leader

Contrary to common belief: Not everything can happen this way
where many people make a fatal mistake: mixing them with processing or randomness. In our culture, especially in business, we only make decisions that can be explained by data and logic. However, this heavy reliance on cold logic limits our ability to work effectively and adapt.

I encourage you to reconsider these beliefs. Logic is very powerful, but it cannot predict the future in difficult and unpredictable situations. There are times when you just don't find meaning and that's when intuition is your best friend.

Deep knowledge is the perfect balance between intelligence and quiet knowledge, but to get there you have to start trusting your intuition. Your brain has learned more than you think. The problem is that for fear of making mistakes we tend to ignore our feelings and prioritize endless analyses.

Amazing Benefits of Trusting Your Intuition
Better and faster decision-making: Intuition helps you make decisions without the need for analytics. In today's ever-changing world, the ability to work quickly is a competitive advantage.

Strong and flexible capability: Deep resolution helps you see beyond. By combining your past experiences, your brain allows you to come up with creative and unique solutions that you can't imagine.

Act effectively in a crisis: When there is pressure, the ability to make quick decisions is essential. Mindfulness helps you navigate a stressful environment without fear or hesitation. Your brain, trained to recognize patterns, knows what to do even if you don't have all the information.

Relationships with others: Intuition also plays an important role in our relationships. Have you ever had feelings for someone, a feeling you couldn't trust? This is your intuition in action, which helps you read social issues faster than if you were based solely on facts.

Personal and professional development: The more you trust your intuition, the easier it will be to improve your decision-making skills. Not only will this make you more effective, but it will also make you a better and more confident leader.

How do you increase confidence in mental thinking?
Now that you know how powerful introspection is, it's time to cultivate it. Here are some practical steps to get started:

Listen to your inner voice: Whenever you make a decision, listen to that inner voice that guides you. Listen to their opinion. Over time, you'll learn to distinguish real ideas from simple, abstract ones.

Do more of what you know: The more you try to expose yourself to new situations, the better your brain will work and create patterns. Regular practice will help you make better decisions.

Meditation and meditation: Meditation and daily meditation can calm your mind and connect you with your thoughts. Mental space is critical for the brain to communicate and make more effective decisions.

Research: After making all the important decisions, think about the process. Why did you make this decision? By understanding how your mind works, you'll strengthen it.

It's time to act
It's time to put aside your doubts and start trusting your heart. Knowledge is not something mysterious or an unattainable skill; It is a skill that can be learned and that can transform your ability to make decisions and face challenges with strength and wisdom. The future is being written and the best way to ensure success is to use your imagination with confidence.

Don't let the fear of making mistakes destroy you! Your brain knows better. Trust it, act now, and take your leadership to the next level.

INFLUENCE AND CONNECTION: LEADING WITH EMPATHY

Most people believe that a good leader is someone who has control over their authority and must be strong, decisive and in many cases does not care about others.

This vision has been passed down from generation to generation: a leader is a powerful person who controls the process and directs the destiny of his team from the top. But today this vision has been abandoned.

Do you know that understanding is one of the most important things a leader can have? Yes, you read that right. Empathy, which is the ability to understand and empathize with others, is now one of the keys to leadership. In a world where speed, efficiency, and connectivity are important, understanding is not only a critical skill, but also an urgent need.

This blog challenges you to rethink what you believe about leadership. Because true leadership is not a feeling, but an understanding. It's time to start leading with your heart and let your emotions become your greatest strength.

Leadership Research: Why Does It Work?
Sympathy is not a good idea in business conversations. It's actually the intelligence associated with the human brain. Neuroscience has shown that a person's emotional connection is one of the most effective sources of human strength and motivation.

In the brain, mirror neurons are responsible for our ability to "hear" what others think. These nerves allow us to put ourselves in other people's shoes and see how they feel as if they were our own. When a leader is empathetic, they activate these neurons in their team, creating an emotional response that strengthens relationships and creates deep and meaningful relationships.

Not only does this make people not trust you, but it also increases collaboration and productivity. When people feel understood, they work with passion and commitment. Empathy is a more powerful tool than strict commands or commands because people are motivated by emotion, not power.

The Challenge of Faith: Compassion Is Not a Weakness

One of the biggest myths about leadership is that it is seen as a weakness. Many people think that to be a good leader you have to be independent, strong and in many cases you don't care about the opinion of others. This idea is wrong.

Leadership with compassion does not mean being soft or giving in to everything, but knowing when to be firm and when to be compassionate. Managers understand that people's emotions are the driving force behind productivity, innovation, and loyalty. And they know how to use this power in a good way.

In fact, opinion leaders are most effective in times of crisis, when emotions are intense and uncertainty hangs in the air. Empathy allows a leader to lead their team through adversity, not only through strategy and logic, but also through teamwork.

Best practices build consensus

1. Improve communication and collaboration

Consensus creates an environment where people feel comfortable expressing their thoughts, ideas, and concerns. When a leader shows understanding and respect for their team's opinions, people are open, willing to voice their opinions, and most importantly, willing to cooperate.

Empathy allows a team to work together, where each member's strengths are combined and problems are faced together. A team that believes in its leader is ready to move on.

2. Increase cooperation and energy

Empathy not only increases acceptance, but it also creates solidarity that can lead to cooperation. When a manager cares about the health of his colleagues, he gives meaning to his work and tells them that his efforts are directly related to success.

This type of leadership fosters genuine motivation, where people work not only to meet external needs, but because they believe in the mission and value of the partnership. Emotions are the most important source of motivation, and good leaders know how to motivate them to perform at their best.

The group leads with good understanding because people feel they have great support. When partners know they can rely on a leader who understands and supports them, they face challenges with confidence and determination.

In difficult times, understanding acts as the glue that holds the team together. Not only does this improve performance during a crisis, but it also improves leadership and creates a workplace where people feel valued and supported.

The Mind of a Leader

Encourage innovation and creativity

Managers don't just manage projects, they foster innovation. When people feel that their opinions are heard and respected, they feel free to experiment, take risks, and think outside the box. Empathy creates an environment where ideas flow and participants become interested in new solutions without fear of judgment.

Leaders who listen to and understand their team's feelings create an environment where innovation becomes the norm. Positive thinking develops when people feel valued by opening up new ways of thinking and problem-solving skills.

The Future of Leadership is Compassion – Act Now

In today's rapidly changing world, successful leaders are not the strongest, but the most compassionate. Empathy is a skill that can change the future of a leader and if you haven't incorporated it into your leadership style, now is the time to do it.

Why wait? The world needs leaders who not only lead, but connect. Leaders understand their teams, give them meaning, motivate them to be better, and show them that they are valued.

Never underestimate the power of empathy. If you want to make an impact, if you want to change the world, start by changing your ways. Start leading with compassion. It's the most powerful way to connect, change, and improve those around you.

It's your turn! Act now to start building a strong, collaborative, and humane future. Empathy: kiss him.

Page 124

James Lass

HOW THE BRAIN INTERPRETS AND RESPONDS TO SOCIAL CONNECTION

The Hidden Power That Drives Your Success

Imagine you're attending an important meeting or perhaps a social event and something inside you tells you that something is wrong. Maybe it's a slight change in someone's tone of voice, or that distant look you get from across the room. How do you know things have changed even if nothing is said?

The answer lies in your brain. The human brain is inherently social, and its ability to reflect relationships, interpret the emotional states of others, and adapt to social interactions is greater than we imagine. Relationships aren't just about feelings; It is a biological, psychological, and profound model for humanity.

Today I'm going to delve into your brain and show you why social interaction isn't just a "complement" to your life, but essential to your success and happiness. Let go of the belief that relationships are just "personal relationships." The ability to communicate with others is the key to personal and professional growth.

The Social Brain: Why Do We Connect?
From the moment we are born, human interaction is central to our lives. Humans are programmed to seek out, recognize, and respond to social cues. We need to live in community and connect with one another. The brain does

not work in isolation, but is distributed, so it constantly interacts with others.

There is a specific area of the brain that is activated whenever we experience meaningful social interactions. When we feel accepted, understood, or connected to others, the reward system (including parts of the brain like the nucleus accumbens) is activated. This process releases dopamine, a positive neurotransmitter that makes us feel good and creates a positive response that encourages us to seek out that relationship more.

In addition, regions involved in processing emotions, such as the amygdala, also play an important role. The amygdala analyzes social cues, detects emotions such as sympathy, anger, or fear, and helps respond quickly to relationships. You have seen His brain not only "feels" human interactions, but interprets and responds to them immediately.

Social Connections and the Brain: The Key to Success
In a world where we are constantly bombarded with information and good communication seems to take up more of our lives, good social connections are more important than ever. True success depends not only on our intellectual or technical abilities, but also on our ability to build strong relationships.

Why? Social interaction not only improves your emotional well-being, but also allows you to make decisions, innovate, and lead.

1. Social interaction can improve your emotional intelligence

When you interact with other people in real life, you understand yourself and others better. Empathy is an important component of emotional intelligence, a brain circuit designed to pick up on the emotional cues of those around you.

Did you know that people with high emotional intelligence make more effective decisions in complex environments? Empathy not only allows you to understand the feelings of others, but also how to respond to those feelings. Leaders who understand this skill can have a profound and real impact on others.

2. Social connections can increase motivation and productivity.

Good communication inspires motivation and increases productivity. When people feel connected, they are more willing to cooperate, give time and energy, and contribute to common goals.

The science backs it up: studies show that when people feel part of a community, their levels of oxytocin (the bonding hormone) increase, giving them a sense of belonging and giving them the energy to keep working hard.

3. Connecting with others increases personal stability

Social connections don't just make us feel good, they also give us strength. Meaningful relationships provide a support system in times of crisis. By feeling supported by others, your brain improves self-care and reduces stress.

When you're stuck, social connections can relieve stress and help you calm down, focus, and stay focused. Additionally, healthy relationships can help improve physical and mental health by reducing cortisol (stress hormone) levels and improving overall health.

4. Relationships can increase your ability to innovate and be creative

Relationships with others can not only provide you with emotional support, but also increase your creativity. The brain is a social component: when you work in a team, share ideas, and interact with people from different backgrounds and perspectives, your mind expands. Social connections improve your problem-solving skills, give you new perspectives and ideas, and support new ideas.

Regular social interaction helps your brain expand, adapt, and connect in new ways. Creativity thrives in an environment where people feel heard and understood. It's the power that can change your life, your career, and your business.

In future relationships: are you ready to act?

It's time to stop thinking that work and relationships are two different worlds. The human brain is designed to function on its own. Every social interaction is an opportunity to strengthen your emotional skills, increase your creativity, and achieve lasting success.

If you want to be more productive, happier, stronger, and more successful, now is the time to start investing in your social media. The brain responds and adapts to the limitations you create. The more you develop these relationships, the stronger your cognitive, emotional, and social skills will become.

Don't make social connections a priority. Whether in your personal or professional life, connecting with others is equally important to your success and well-being. Act now. Build real relationships, invest in a support network, and watch your brain respond to propel you to new levels of success, creativity, and happiness.

The future is created today, through connections! Connect, grow, and change your life.

James Lass

THE NEUROSCIENCE OF EMPATHY AND ITS IMPACT ON TEAMS

The Secret Key to Transforming Performance

Imagine a team that not only works together, but deeply understands each other. A group where each member feels that their voice is heard, that their feelings are understood and that their efforts are appreciated not only with words, but also with the real commitment of their peers. How does it feel to be part of a team like this? What if I told you that, from a scientific point of view, these teams have the ability to change not only the results, but also the organizational culture?

This is where the neuroscience of empathy comes into play. Being able to put yourself in someone else's shoes, pick up on other people's feelings, and respond authentically isn't just a social skill; It's a powerful nerve tool that drives performance, innovation, and prosperity in any team. And no, it is not just about "good intentions" or "sentimentality"; That's science.

In this blog, I'll explain how your brain and your partner's brain respond to empathy and how this skill can make the difference between an average team and an unstoppable team. It's time to challenge old beliefs, dispel misconceptions about leadership and productivity, and start changing your team dynamics.

Cognitive Science: Why Does It Work?
Compassion is not just an abstract value or a gesture of kindness. It is a biological response that is integrated into the structure of our brain. When we communicate with

other people, the human brain doesn't just process the words we hear or observe other people's behavior. Read the feelings. Feeling other people's inner states. And this happens so quickly and directly that many times we don't even realize it.

This happens because of mirror neurons. These brain cells act like a mirror, reflecting and processing other people's emotions. When a team member smiles, expresses frustration, or even sadness, your brain responds by activating the same areas of the brain that would be activated if it were you. Yes! It's hard to understand in your biology!

How will this affect the team? When people have empathy, they connect emotionally. This sense of connection not only improves interpersonal relationships, but also fosters trust and cooperation. The understanding of the team is a more cohesive, engaged, and effective team.

Surprising Benefits of Understanding in Teams

1. Trust and good communication

When a team member feels that their feelings and attitudes are understood, they trust their colleagues more. This trust translates directly into more open and honest communication. Instead of fearing judgment or conflict, people are comfortable sharing ideas, expressing opinions, and resolving disagreements constructively.

Science backs it up: research shows that teams with high levels of empathy are 60% more likely to resolve

Page 132

conflicts effectively and maintain fluid communication without always becoming a battleground.

2. Increase productivity and performance

One of the most common beliefs in the workplace is that intense competition and high expectations are the keys to performance. However, empathic relationships can be strengthened. When team members feel valued, listened to, and supported, their motivation and engagement will increase dramatically.

Neuroscience shows that oxytocin, known as the "loyalty hormone" or "love hormone," is released in large amounts when we empathize with each other. This neurotransmitter not only improves our ability to work in a team, but also reduces stress and increases our ability to concentrate, which leads to better performance.

Empathetic teams are 40% more likely to exceed their performance goals because they are motivated by shared goals and emotional cohesion.

3. Increase innovation and creativity

Emotionally connected teams are more creative and innovative. Because? Because when people feel heard and accepted, they feel safer sharing new ideas, even the most dangerous or unusual ones. Compassion creates an environment where weaknesses are not seen as weaknesses, but as opportunities to grow and learn.

Science shows that empathy activates areas of the brain associated with problem-solving and decision-making, increasing the creativity of collaborative teams. Insightful

The Mind of a Leader

team members feel they can come up with innovative solutions without fear of rejection.

4. Improve the overall well-being of the team

Self-compassion not only affects performance, but also the emotional well-being of individuals. Affective interactions reduce levels of cortisol, the stress hormone, which reduces fatigue and anxiety. Teams that practice empathy have employee turnover rates of less than 50% and enjoy higher levels of job satisfaction. Who wouldn't want to be part of a team that not only achieves goals, but also cares about others?

Busting the myth: compassion is not weakness, it is strength
A common misconception is that being compassionate means being kind or patient. Nothing could be further from the truth. Compassion is not the same as weakness. In fact, compassionate leaders are more respected, more effective, and better able to lead in times of crisis.
Why? Because empathy strengthens the resilience of the team. When someone feels understood and emotionally supported, they are more likely to stick together in the face of difficult challenges. Empathy provides the emotional foundation that allows teams to stay calm, face fear and adversity.

Your Call to Action: Embrace Empathy Today
It's time to break away from old ideas about how to build high-performing teams. Empathy is a smart strategy, not a luxury. Teams led with empathy can overcome obstacles more effectively, work more efficiently, and are more motivated to succeed.

Page 134

Now it's time to take the next step. Start developing empathy in your team: learn to listen carefully, acknowledge others' feelings, and respond authentically. The results will be incredible! You will see how your team can become a determined, proactive and innovative department that achieves previously unattainable goals.

It's time to rule your heart. The neuroscience of compassion is on your side and now you too can be part of the change that will change the world. Act now. Let empathy be your most powerful leadership tool. Because in the business world as well as in life itself, relationships are the true power that leads us to success.

CREATING PSYCHOLOGICALLY SAFE ENVIRONMENTS

The Quiet Revolution That Drives Success

Imagine this: a workplace where everyone is valued, where ideas flow freely, where you can be vulnerable without fear of judgment, and where every team member knows they have the right to disagree, to learn, and to grow without negative consequences. Is this a good place to work? Now think about it, this type of environment not only improves the quality of life of individuals, but also promotes the productivity of the entire group. The question is: why don't we do this?

Creating a safe environment is nothing new, nor is it a "good" thing that companies "should" do. There are biological and neurological requirements for normal functioning. If you want your team to be more productive, more knowledgeable, focused, and engaged, the most important thing is to create an environment where everyone feels safe. Science proves it and today I'm going to show you why and how you can start changing that today.

The Science of Curing Mental Illness: Why Does It Work?
Imagine that every time you speak in a group, you're worried that you'll be laughed at and ignored. How do you think this affects your creativity? Or do you want to share a smart solution? You're likely to give in, hide your emotions, and get carried away instead of expressing your unique ideas. An emotionally insecure place may seem like this.

The human brain is designed to perceive evil. Whenever we see something negative, the amygdala (the part of the brain that controls emotional responses) kicks in and issues a warning. If you feel like your ideas are being ignored, laughed at, or misunderstood, your brain is in trouble. Not only will this make you feel better, but it will also affect your mental abilities. Stress and fear can inhibit our ability to think clearly and inhibit our ability to work, be creative, and solve problems.

Now imagine that the environment is different. In a safe psychological environment, you won't be afraid to express your ideas or make mistakes. Your brain is not in a state of obstruction, but in a state of growth, where ideas flow unhindered and collaboration is not judged. This not only encourages creativity but also unlocks latent potential.

Amazing Benefits of Creating a Safe Environment

1. Promotes innovation and creativity
Groups can express their ideas safely without fear of being rejected by the group's creativity. Why? Because it requires creativity. If you're worried that your ideas will be mocked or dismissed, you can't speak up. But in a safe environment, ideas can flow. Team members can try new ideas, make mistakes, and learn without negative consequences.

Companies with a safe psychological environment are 35% more likely to create new ideas and 45% more likely to implement them. Can you imagine what your team would do if they worked without fear?

2. Improve work performance and profitability
Fear and stress are the enemies of work. When people feel that their ideas and contributions are important, it doesn't mean they'll work hard; They did a great job. They are passionate, thoughtful, and willing to overcome obstacles.

Scientific research shows that groups with psychological safety perform 30% better than groups without psychological safety. Social activism increases significantly when people feel they can express their opinions without being judged.

3. Strengthen interpersonal relationships and teamwork
In an emotionally safe environment, not only do positive thoughts occur, but interpersonal relationships are strengthened. When team members show vulnerability and share their thoughts and feelings without fear, a strong foundation of trust is built. People begin to work

The Mind of a Leader

together, recognizing the unique value each person brings to the team.

Trust is the glue that holds a team together, without it you won't be able to perform at your best, no matter how talented you are. A safe space is a place where people can open up and work together, not individually, but as a cohesive team. Improve quality of life, reduce daylight saving time

Creating a safe environment not only affects the quality of work, but also affects the health of workers. Chronic stress from adverse or negative environments can lead to fatigue, anxiety, depression, and chronic illness.

When people work in an environment where they feel accepted and supported, their cortisol levels (the stress hormone) are reduced, improving physical and mental health. This not only increases the well-being of workers, but also reduces the number of workers and improves the overall working environment.

Act Now: How to Create an Emotionally Safe Environment?

Great question: How do you start creating a psychologically safe environment within your team or company? Here are some important steps you can take now:

1. Encourage Open and Open Communication

The key to emotional safety is openness. As a leader, it's important to show vulnerability. Share your questions and challenges. Make sure everyone, including leaders, is always learning. When people see that you're vulnerable, too, they're more likely to share their thoughts and feelings.

2. Learn to actively listen

Love is an important component of emotional security. Practice active listening: Ask open-ended questions, acknowledge what others are hearing, and make sure everyone has a chance to speak. Listening without judgment is what people enjoy the most.

3. Celebrate failure as an opportunity for growth

The fear of failure is one of the biggest obstacles in the work environment. Change the narrative: celebrate failure as an opportunity to learn and grow. When people know that failure will not be punished, but seen as a lesson, innovation and experimentation skyrocket.

4. Set shared standards

As a team, it's important that you set clear standards of mutual respect. This includes respecting the opinions of others, not tolerating insults or disrespect, and providing constructive rather than destructive feedback.

5. Strengthen trust and transparency

Trust is built day by day. Take concrete steps to demonstrate your commitment to psychological safety: stay open to decisions, listen to your team, and show that their well-being is your priority.

Change starts now

Don't wait any longer. If you want your team to be more creative, more collaborative, happier, and more productive, creating a psychologically safe environment is not an option, but an urgent need. Companies that implement this type of culture are market-leading companies, high-performing companies, and companies that retain employee loyalty and engagement.

The future of your organization depends on the emotional and psychological safety you can create today. Get started now, take the first step in changing your culture, and watch your team become stronger and more successful.

Take action: Create psychological safety and unleash your team's potential.

James Lass

STRESS MANAGEMENT AND LEADER RESILIENCE

The Secret to Mastering Adversity and Elevating Your Leadership

What's the difference between a boss who crumbles under pressure and a person who grows stronger under pressure? Why do some leaders seem to thrive in the face of adversity, while others collapse in the storm? The answer is not magic or luck. A very powerful product, scientifically proven for everyone: stress and energy management.

Imagine yourself as the leader of a team, faced with difficult decisions, endless deadlines, and high expectations. The pressure continues. But don't give in to these pressures, get up, stay calm and lead your team to victory. This is the power of the boss. Best of all: this power is within you, waiting to be unleashed.

Today I'm going to help you change your mind. We dispel common misconceptions about stress and learn how the world's best leaders overcome stress and build resilience. This is more than just a call to action; A sudden call to change the way we lead and face challenges with unwavering courage.

Stress: The hidden enemy that can make you big or knock you down
We've all heard that stress is bad, right? There is a common belief that stress is something to be avoided, as it can reduce productivity, health, and quality of life.

The Mind of a Leader

Surprisingly, the truth is, if handled properly, stress can lead to success. The problem is not the stress itself, but how we deal with it.

The human brain is designed to cope with stress. When faced with anger, the brain initiates the fight-or-flight response, releasing cortisol and adrenaline, which increases energy and generates energy. This protective mechanism has been critical to our survival for thousands of years. If managed properly, stress can improve decision-making, increase motivation, and improve performance.

But what happens when you're stressed? If we don't know how to take care of ourselves, stress can turn into fatigue, anxiety, and mental exhaustion. A boss who doesn't know how to handle stress will likely get angry, conflicted, and unproductive. This is where strength comes in: the ability to recover quickly from problems that arise.

Resilience: The Secret Power of Great Leaders

Practice
Resilience is more than just "getting through" difficult times; it is the ability to succeed in spite of it; The bottom line is that, like stress, it's not something we're born with, it's something we can learn from. Yes! As a leader, you have the ability to be confident and effective.
How does resistance develop? Neuroscience tells us that the brain is plastic, which means it can change over time. Sustainability is created through actions and thoughts. A courageous leader is not someone who never fails, but someone who gets up after falling. Good leaders do not

avoid problems, but rather empower them to deal with them with wisdom and intelligence.

Sustainability is driven by four key pillars:

Growth mindset: Sustainability leaders see challenges as learning opportunities. Even if they encounter problems, they won't blame external things or give up. They believe they can learn and change over time. These thoughts are a way to cope with chronic anxiety.

Emotions: Confidence starts with knowing and understanding your emotions. A leader who knows his own inner feelings can control his emotions and prevent others from caring about him.

Psychological resilience: Sustainable leaders change rapidly. They will not follow the same path or be blocked by obstacles. Like water: flexible, able to find new paths and adapt to new situations.

Social support and networks of trust: resilience is not just about work. The support of a team, mentor or close circle is crucial to overcome difficulties. Confident leaders know that there is no shame in asking for help.

The Incredible Benefits of Stress Management and Mindfulness

1. Improve decision-making under pressure
Leaders who learn to manage stress can make quick and effective decisions under pressure. When the brain is deprived of cortisol, important tasks such as decision-making, planning, and decision-making become more efficient.

2. Improve team effectiveness

A confident leader inspires his team. Team members feel safe and motivated when they see their leaders staying strong and resilient in the face of challenges. A team whose leader is under constant pressure is an engaged and productive team.

3. Improve physical and mental health

Chronic stress is the secret enemy of health. Stress management and strength training not only help improve performance but also reduce the risk of stress-related conditions such as high blood pressure, fatigue, and anxiety. Courageous leaders live long, healthy lives.

Courageous leaders are not discouraged by failure, but learn from it. This continued growth fosters a culture of innovation throughout the organization. Strong leaders encourage experimentation and are willing to take calculated risks.

Call to Action: Turn Stress into Power!
Stress management and resilience aren't just optional skills; It is the skill that separates good leaders from great leaders. If you want to realize your potential as a leader, it's time to take action. Stress can be your worst enemy, but it can also be your best teacher. Would you dare to take it and turn it into a powerful weapon?

Here's what you can do today:

Exercise your mind: Practice meditation, mindfulness, or any method that calms your mind and reduces stress.

Adopt a growth mindset: Every obstacle is an opportunity. Learn from your failures and use each failure as a way to improve.

Create a support network: Don't face challenges and difficulties alone. Ask mentors, friends, and colleagues to help you stand your ground.

Make self-care a priority: Resilience is impossible without physical and mental health. Exercise, eat well, sleep and most importantly, take care of your health.

The future of your leadership depends on your ability to cope with stress and recover. Don't wait any longer. Start training your mind now to suppress the opponent, not the enemy. The leader in you is waiting to be awakened.

Awaken your courage and become the leader your team needs!

HOW STRESS AFFECTS THE BRAIN AND DECISION-MAKING

A Call to Unleash Your Potential

Stress, a constant companion in modern life, has a negative power that many people do not understand. We see it every day: stress surrounds us, consumes us, and depresses us. But have you ever stopped to think about how stress affects your brain and your decisions?

The Mind of a Leader

Here's a shocking truth you've never been told: stress not only makes your life worse, it affects your ability to make effective decisions. But if the leader cannot make clear and correct decisions, the future of his team and his company will be in danger.

This is not an article about "stress management." It's a difficult decision to understand how your brain can be affected in ways you can't imagine and how it affects your work, your leadership, and your life. But the most powerful thing about all of this is that you can change it.

Today I'm going to show you how stress affects the brain, why it affects decision-making, and what you can do right now to change it and regain your power. It's time to take control.

Anxiety: The Invisible Enemy of Decisions
Imagine: you're in a big meeting, there's an important decision on the table. Stress starts to build: pressure on deadlines, team expectations, uncertainty about the outcome. Your brain begins to react. The amygdala, the small part of the brain that controls emotions and responses to life, kicks in.

Stress activates the first biological response: "fight or flight." At that point, your brain is ready to respond immediately to the threat. Stress hormones, such as cortisol and adrenaline, are released into your system. It gives your body strength to face problems. However, the price of such a reaction is that it removes the main parts of your brain, which are responsible for making good decisions, planning for the long term, and thinking critically.

Page 146

What happens in the brain under stress?
In times of stress, your brain goes into "survival" mode. This means that the most complex and logical functions of the brain, such as the prefrontal cortex, responsible for decision-making, self-regulation and problem solving, are inhibited. Meanwhile, the amygdala, responsible for our emotional responses, takes over.

This shift in priorities has important implications for decision-making. Instead of considering the best option or considering the consequences, you make decisions out of fear or panic. The result? Irrational decisions, instead of moving forward, will keep you stuck in a cycle of stress, reaction instead of strategy.

And that's not all. Chronic stress damages the brain and affects areas related to memory and learning. In the long term, the brain works less under stress. It is becoming more and more difficult to have a clear vision and make the right decision.

Science: How decisions sabotage stress
According to scientific studies, chronic stress can reduce the ability of the prefrontal cortex to plan, make long-term decisions, and evaluate the right options. Instead, emotional reactions drive decision-making. Your brain seems to be working in automatic mode, making random decisions.

Here's a surprise: stress doesn't just affect your decision-making in times of trouble. As stress increases over time, the ability to think clearly and rationally decreases. It can lead to errors in judgment, rash decisions, and a lack of

The Mind of a Leader

shortcuts. In short, stress robs you of the ability to be an effective strategic leader.

Direct influence on leadership: How does it affect your decision to act as a leader?
If you're a leader, the feeling will run deeper. Your decisions not only affect you, but your entire team, your company, your organization. A leader under pressure not only makes good decisions, but also communicates them to their team, which affects the entire process.

Concerns you'll face:

Avoid making decisions: The fear of making wrong decisions will disappear.
Irrational decision-making: Instead of considering all options, you rely on speed and pressure.
React to emotions: Instead of reacting rationally, you react based on the fear or excitement of the moment.
Not delegating well: Micromanaging leaders can lead to stress, which reduces team creativity and strength.
Not only does it make you angry, but it also causes a lot of bad decisions and more stress. A leader who makes poor decisions under pressure loses the trust of his team, which increases team stress and overall uncertainty.

Solution: How to Turn Stress into a Tool for Success
Stress is not the enemy. If you know how to manage it, you can use it as a fast, productive and beautiful tool. Here are the main steps to turning stress into a tool for success:

1. Take a deep breath and control your immediate response

Deep breathing activates the parasympathetic nervous system, which seeks to relieve stress. Taking deep breaths when you're stressed will help you regain control of your frontal cortex, allowing you to think clearly before making rash decisions.

2. Practice mindfulness to restore inner peace
Meditation allows you to be present and aware without thinking or feeling. This practice can help you identify emotional reactions before they take over, allowing you to choose a more strategic response.

3. Learn how to share and inspire your team
When you're under pressure, it's easy to improvise. But effective leaders delegate responsibilities and trust their teams. Delegating tasks frees up your attention, allowing you to make important decisions and reduce stress.

4. Make decisions based on facts rather than emotions.
To prevent this from happening, make sure you make decisions based on facts and factual information rather than emotional impulses. Create a process to review all options before taking action.

5. Acceptance: Learning from mistakes
Recognizing that mistakes are part of the growth process is key to reducing the stress that causes fear and anxiety. Strong leaders see failures as learning opportunities, not threats.

Take action now and turn stress into determination!
Stress shouldn't be your enemy. With the right tools, you can control it and use it to your advantage. Now that you know how stress affects your thinking and decision-

making, you have the knowledge you need to act with clarity, confidence, and strategy.

It's time to stop being a jerk and start using it as a powerful tool. Take control now: Start with deep breathing, mindfulness, and mindful decision-making. Your team, company and future will thank you.

STRATEGIES FOR STAYING CALM AT KEY MOMENTS

The Secret Power of Successful Leaders

What distinguishes an exceptional leader from an average leader? Is it knowledge? Technical skills? These are important times. Those moments of anxiety when everything seems to fall apart and uncertainty surrounds everything. The key difference between successful leaders and those who are not is their ability to remain calm.

Have you ever heard of the trap in trouble? The feeling that time stands still, decisions become difficult, the mind begins to spin, and thoughts keep crashing. What many don't realize is that in situations like these, staying calm is not just an emotional issue, but an important skill that can be trained. Once you master this skill, you will be an unstoppable leader.

This blog shares scientific and practical strategies for staying calm when it matters most and shows how the power of calm can transform your ability to make decisions, lead teams, and achieve success. We'll dispel common beliefs about stress and anxiety and show that staying calm isn't just a good habit, it's a practical skill you need to learn to master. It's time to take the next step towards a better version of the manager!

Why is it so difficult to stay calm in a crisis?
. Before we get into it, it's important to understand why the human brain loses its cool during times of high stress. The answer lies in the neuroscience of stress.

When you're faced with a difficult problem, such as an important idea, a business problem, or an important decision, your brain comes alive. The amygdala, the part of the brain that activates when there is danger, sends signals to the body to prepare to "fight or flight." The prefrontal cortex, the area responsible for planning and rational decision-making, suffers because the brain prioritizes survival over decision-making.

This biological process is completely normal. It is a living legacy. However, what many people don't know is that you can train your brain not to allow this behavior to control your behavior.

Key Strategies for Staying Calm: Let Your Mind Lead in the Face of Challenges
If you want to lead confidently and effectively, you need to learn how to handle pressure. Here I offer practical strategies that will not only calm you down in difficult situations, but also help you make quick, smart, and practical decisions.

Deep breathing is a simple and effective way to restore calm during stressful times. When stress activates the amygdala, your body is flooded with adrenaline and

The Mind of a Leader

cortisol. Deep breathing counteracts this process by calming the nerves and activating the prefrontal cortex, the part of the brain responsible for rational decision-making.
How are you? Try the 4-7-8 technique:

Breathe in for 4 seconds
Hold for 7 seconds.
Breathe slowly for 8 seconds
This simple exercise can change your mind completely and help you think clearly about the storm.

Instead of worrying about what could go wrong, meditation brings you back to the present moment, allowing you to make decisions based on reality rather than fear or preconceived notions.

How to apply it? Try to observe your thoughts and feelings without judging them. If you're feeling tired, wake up and accept your feelings instead of letting them control your actions. This simple act of awareness can suppress the brain's fight-or-flight response.

Change your attitude: turn fear into action
Fear is the leading cause of stress in difficult times. But fear isn't real, it's your brain's idea of the unknown. Changing your mindset means changing the story you have in mind: instead of seeing a problem as a threat, you start seeing it as an opportunity to grow, innovate, or learn something new.

Practice this: Whenever you find yourself in a difficult moment, ask yourself, "What can I learn from this? How can I grow from this experience?" By changing your way of thinking, you turn fear into power.

Page 152

Decision Tree Technique

Moments of uncertainty are often surrounded by a cloud of choices and decisions. The "tree" technique is a simple way to visualize and organize the decision-making process. Writing down options and solutions will help you clarify the picture and find a path forward.

How does it work? Draw a decision tree with possible branches. As you analyze each one, write down the results and evaluate the pros and cons. This practice breaks down stress into manageable steps, reducing feelings of burnout.

5. Building resilience: learning from every mistake

Great leaders don't always fail, but they learn from their failures and become stronger. Patience helps you stay calm even when things go wrong. Each question is a lesson for the future.

Action: Whenever you encounter a problem, stop and reflect on what you've learned. Eliminate stress and allow your mind to focus on learning and not on fear.

6. Trust your team: Teamwork generates stress

Stressful times should not be faced alone. Allowing and trusting your team not only reduces their emotional burden but also increases teamwork and productivity. Trusting others can save you unnecessary stress and allow you to focus on what's important.

Tip: Make sure your team knows they can trust you and others. Confidence allows you to stay calm in any situation.

Incredible benefits of having peace of mind

1. Improves decision-making: When you are calm, your prejudices are activated and your ability to think and think rationally improves.

2. Reduce chronic stress: Being calm can reduce cortisol, improving your long-term health and well-being.

3. Creative ability: Silent leaders have the ability to make quick and effective decisions, making the process faster and more efficient.

4. Keep your attitude strong: When you stay calm in the important moments, you will be strong and confident in your ability to face any challenge.

It's time to work!
What you just read is more than a theory; It is an unstoppable path to leadership. Whenever you are faced with a critical moment, remember that patience is a skill that can be developed. This is not a luxury, but an important strategy for good decision-making, leadership, and success.

Now it's time to implement these ideas! The next time you encounter stress, don't let it control you. Take a deep breath, stay calm, and make stress your best friend.

Your future leadership starts now.

Page 154

James Lass

CULTIVATING RESILIENCE AS A LEADER

Your Secret Superpower

Did you know that your ability to get back up after a fall is more important than the number of falls? In the world of leadership, success is not measured by achievements, but by the strength you show in the face of failure, challenge, and adversity.

Now you're probably thinking, "I'm not Superman!" How can you stay strong when everything is broken?" The truth is that perseverance is not a talent that is born, but a skill that we can all cultivate. The good news is: once you develop it, your leadership skills will be unstoppable.

Today I'm going to show you how to gain the power to not only survive in stressful times, but also to be alive, inspire your team, and achieve the success that others only dream of. Along the way, we challenge some common beliefs and reveal the scientific secrets behind how the brain and body help us overcome obstacles. So if you're ready to change your leadership, read on. Resilience is not an option, it is a necessity for true success!

What is resilience?
It is not about being able to withstand adversity or endure hardships. It's more than that. The ability to adapt, grow, and strengthen with every challenge. A strong leader is not someone who can't fail, but someone who will rise and come back stronger, brighter, and stronger than ever.

The Mind of a Leader

But how can we build our own resistance? First, we need to understand how our brains work when we face challenges.

The Science of Resilience: How the Brain Overcomes Adversity

The human brain is designed to overcome challenges. When we experience anger or stress, the brain activates the amygdala, which controls the fight-or-flight response. This is a genetic survival mechanism that makes us respond to adversity. However, when stress persists, your ability to make sound decisions is affected and your brain begins to enter a state of mental exhaustion and fatigue.

This is where resistance magic comes into play. Your brain has an amazing ability to adapt and renew itself, called neuroplasticity. As you face and overcome challenges, your brain rearranges connections to make you stronger. This means that every crisis not only teaches you something important, but also prepares you better for the future.

Not only can the brain cope with stress, but it can also learn to cope better and cope with difficult situations over time. Most importantly, resilience is the result of training your mind to be stronger in every challenge.

Challenging Common Beliefs About Wellness
Many people believe that being healthy means not experiencing pain or stress. But this is not true. Resilience is not the absence of pain, but the ability to face pain and move forward. A strong leader is not one who is not afraid, but one who acts in spite of fear.

Page 156

Another myth is resilience. But it's not about being "indestructible," it's about flexibility, adaptability, and the ability to learn from every experience. In fact, the strongest leaders are the humble ones who recognize their weaknesses and use those lessons to grow rather than hide them.

Resilience is not something you have, it is something you cultivate.

5 Strategies to Develop a Leader's Mind

If you want to be a strong leader, the good news is that you can train your brain to be stronger when faced with challenges. Here are five key strategies to achieve just that.

1. Develop a growth mindset.
Thinking is the key to survival. When your mind is stuck, you think you have little ability to handle stress or overcome challenges. But if you adopt a growth mindset, you'll see every challenge as an opportunity to learn and improve. Don't see yourself as someone who is affected by circumstances, but as someone who has the ability to adapt, learn, and move forward.

How do you implement it? Whenever you face a challenge, ask yourself this question: "What can I learn from this? How can we improve our approach in the future?" This mindset will empower you and help you focus your energy on solutions rather than problems.

2. Strengthen your psychology.
Strong leaders control their emotions. It's not about repressing your emotions, but about understanding and managing them properly. Emotional intelligence allows

you to recognize when stress is affecting you and take steps to avoid it.

Practice: Write a daily list of your emotions. Think about the most stressful time of your day and ask yourself, "Why am I like this?" "How can I best handle these situations?" Emotional intelligence allows you to act in a controlled way instead of impulsive reactions.

3. Build a Support Network
No one can be a leader alone. Being resilient doesn't mean doing it all yourself. Strong leaders surround themselves with a team of mentors, loyal colleagues, and a dedicated team that supports them. Not only will these people provide you with emotional support, but they will also provide you with valuable information and creative solutions that you may not have thought of.

Tip: Make collaboration a central part of your leadership. Realize that your team's strengths are your strengths.

4. Teach compassion and flexibility
Sensitive leaders know not to judge their worth. Self-love is key. Allow yourself to make mistakes and be your best friend instead of self-destructing. Simplicity is also important. Instead of giving up when things don't go as planned, correct course and find new solutions.

5. *Tip:* When faced with failure, repeat to yourself, "Failure is normal. I will learn from him and move forward with more wisdom." Regular exercise, a healthy diet, enough rest, and mindfulness can do a lot for your mind and body. These habits can reduce the effects of stress and give you the strength you need to stay strong during difficult times.

Don't underestimate the power of a good night's sleep or a short walk to clear your mind. Your resilience depends on your physical and mental health.

Courage is not optional: it is the key to your success
As a leader, courage is the skill that separates you from mediocrity. It gives you the strength to not only overcome challenges, but also thrive in them. Building resilience allows you to make clear decisions, build trust in your team, and be strong in any situation.

If you're ready to change your leadership style, implement proactive strategies today. The road to success is full of challenges, but every obstacle is an opportunity to show your inner strength.

It's time to stand up and lead boldly! The next challenge will be your chance to shine. Your success starts now.

THE IMPACT OF CORPORATE CULTURE ON THE BRAIN

How to Transform Your Business from the Inside

Have you ever wondered why some companies always seem to take the next step while others struggle to stay in business? The answer is not only in the numbers or in the business strategy. It's one of those deeper things we don't see often: corporate culture.

But not "letter values" or word incentives in the corridor. A collaborative culture has a direct and measurable impact on our brain chemistry and, in turn, on our performance, health, and most importantly, the overall functioning of the family. Why? Because the human brain is connected to the environment and society. And what happens in a company's culture happens in the head of each employee.

Today I bring you something new: corporate culture not only determines the success of the company, but also shapes the brains of its employees. From the decision-making process, the problem-solving process and the innovation process. I promise that the results will last longer than you think.

What is corporate culture and why is it so powerful?
. Public culture is not just a collection of values or an image of the body. More than that. It is a set of beliefs, behaviors, and feelings that permeate all actions and

decision-making within an organization. Culture, whether conscious or unconscious, is the emotional and social environment in which we operate every day.

This is where neuroscience comes in. The human brain is designed to adapt and respond to the environment. Every time we interact with our partner, we receive emotional information that activates important brain functions related to stress, reward, motivation, and empathy.

Imagine working at a company with a culture that promotes fierce competition, destructive criticism, and a focus on results. Your brain is always on high alert, releasing stress hormones like cortisol. Not only does this harm your mental health, but it also reduces your ability to make good decisions, makes you work harder, and reduces your ability to innovate.

On the other hand, in a positive, inclusive, and cooperative culture where trust is the norm, the brain has high levels of oxytocin, the "trust hormone." This makes you feel confident, more creative, and above all, willing to share your ideas and take risks related to innovation.

How does corporate culture act on the brain?
. The brain, a biological marvel, is very plastic. This means that we adapt and change according to our experiences. And the emotions of our work culture have a direct impact on how our brains communicate and respond to problems.

A culture of trust = more creativity and effective decision-making
When you feel safe in your workplace, your brain releases oxytocin, which is associated with trust and

empathy. Oxytocin promotes cooperation and reduces fear, opening the way to creativity and innovation.

Employees who work in an environment where they feel supported and trusted are more likely to face challenges, share ideas without fear of judgment, and work together effectively. This translates into better decision-making because they are not paralyzed by the fear of failure. It's a good way: a good environment creates a productive brain, which generates good results for the company.

Toxic competitive culture = chronic stress and poor decision-making

Conversely, if you work in a competitive environment and the fear of making mistakes is in the air, your brain is in the defense mechanism, releasing the hormone cortisol. This chronic stress will reduce your ability to make good decisions because your brain is more focused on health than thinking.

In the long term, chronic stress can lead to physical and mental fatigue, reduced fertility, and unlimited decisions out of fear or anxiety. Your creativity dies and creativity becomes a dangerous process, full of internal tension. Freedom is lost because the mind is not open to change, it is closed to fear.

Collaborative culture = greater intelligence and better results

Teams that work in a collaborative environment always perform better. In this environment, there is an increase in dopamine production in the brains of workers, which increases positive social behavior and makes people feel rewarded for working together.

Page 162

A collaborative culture that is inclusive and respectful improves the intelligence of leaders and team members. This increases empathy, the ability to respond to others' opinions without reacting, and constructive conflict resolution. As a result, the team feels connected and motivated to achieve their goals.

Contrary to common sense: culture is not a 'bonus'

Shared culture is not an 'extra' or a 'bonus'. This is the lifeblood of your business. And no, you can't leave it to chance. Culture has a direct impact on the mental and emotional health of your employees. And here's a big revelation: Culture affects mental health and productivity. If you want your team to perform at the highest level, you need to invest in a culture that promotes trust, teamwork, and emotional well-being.

In fact, research shows that companies that create inspiring, inclusive, and emotionally safe environments are 30% more productive, 40% less profitable, and 50% more innovative than companies with toxic or apathetic cultures.

How to Change Company Culture: Act Fast

If you've convinced yourself that culture has a real impact on the way your team thinks, it's time to take action. Here are three key steps to changing company culture from within:

Building trust and open communication

A place where employees can express their opinions and concerns without fear of judgment. Open and transparent communication promotes trust and cooperation, which are essential elements of an emotionally safe environment.

The Mind of a Leader

Mutually beneficial cooperation, not just competition
Change "all for all" to "for the benefit of all". It encourages cooperation, collaboration, and relationship building within the company. Be sure to celebrate success as a team, not as individuals.

Investing in emotional and mental health
Offer wellness programs to help your employees manage stress and maintain a healthy emotional balance. A healthy brain is a productive brain, and a culture that supports employee well-being translates into innovation and performance.

Corporate culture is not a trivial matter: it is your most valuable asset
Today he learned that corporate culture is not an "extra layer" of good value. It's the invisible force that shapes your team's mindset and performance. If you don't, you'll miss out on a golden opportunity to transform your company.
Well, it's time to act. Your company has a huge opportunity waiting to open up, and that opportunity starts with creating a culture that's not just about the numbers, but about the human brain that makes it possible.

Make your corporate culture a powerful engine of innovation, collaboration and excellence! Your team and company will thank you.

Page 164

James Lass

HOW THE ENVIRONMENT AFFECTS OUR NEURAL CONNECTIONS

The Science That Can Change Your Life

Did you know that your environment has the power to change the shape of your brain? What seems difficult or unclear is the science behind neuroscience. Where you work, the people you work with, and even the smallest things in your daily life can change your brain in ways you can't imagine.

This is a surprising fact, but I challenge you to think about something important: you can control your environment to use your brain's capabilities in limitless ways. And what happens in your brain affects everything: your performance, your creativity, your immunity, your ability to make decisions, and most of all your happiness and health.

Today we'll look at how the environment can change the shape of your network and how you can use this powerful information to change your life and your work!

The brain: an organism plain and simple
Let me first address a belief. The brain is not a permanent organ. It was long believed that the brain's neural connections remain intact into adulthood. He's a legend! The brain is very plastic, which means it can change, adapt, and change throughout life.

This ability is called neuroplasticity and therefore our brain not only responds to what we learn, but also adapts to the environment. What you see, hear, touch, smell and, above all, the emotions you experience, affect the growth of your neurons and their connections. The virtual world has the power to rewrite connections in the brain.

How does this process work?
The human brain is made up of billions of interconnected neurons that use electrical signals and signals. Thanks to these relationships, we can learn, answer questions, manage emotions and develop skills. But, interestingly, these relationships don't last long.

When you live in a positive and rich environment, full of mental and health challenges, your brain becomes more connected. Neural networks develop, cognitive abilities increase, memory improves, and creativity increases.

On the other hand, if you're surrounded by a negative or stressful environment, your nervous system may weaken, your cognitive abilities will grind to a halt, and your brain will enter a cycle of self-defense. Prolonged stress, neglect, or lack of energy can damage cells and prevent the growth of new neurons.

A positive environment: your neuroplasticity engine
A positive environment grows the brain. What does a healthy environment imply? Everything active and constructive feeds your mind:

Healthy Relationships: The human brain thrives when it is surrounded by supportive relationships. Oxytocin, known as the "love hormone," is released when we connect well with others, creating a safe environment.

This interaction not only improves your emotional health, but also facilitates learning and decision-making.

Problem stimulation: A problem-loving brain keeps you focused and motivated. The stress and positive experiences we experience when we overcome a problem or learn something new activate parts of the brain associated with problem-solving, innovation, and creativity.

Rich environment: A stimulating environment where you can acquire new ideas, learning, and experiences that support brain development. Continuous learning (whether through books, classes, or deep conversations) leads to the creation of new networks that connect the mind and develop it.

Meditation and recreation: The brain also needs time to relax. An environment that favors meditation, adequate rest, and relaxation allows the brain to recover, which improves thinking and decision-making.

The effects of a bad environment: decreased brain capacity
On the other hand, a bad environment slows you down and affects your brain health more than you think. There are many reasons for these effects:

Chronic stress: Chronic stress increases the level of cortisol in the body, which inhibits neuroplasticity. Too much cortisol can damage brain cells in key areas such as the hippocampus, affecting memory, learning, and decision-making.

The Mind of a Leader

Toxic Environment: A toxic relationship or a negative work environment generates stress and mistrust. This inhibits the brain's ability to think effectively and efficiently, so it chooses to be impulsive and defensive. Instead of creating new connections, the brain remains in a constant state of alertness.

Lack of mental stimulation: The brain needs new experiences and challenges. If it doesn't match what motivates or inspires you, it goes into automatic mode and "exits," losing the ability to adapt to new situations or learn new things.

The power to change your environment to change your brain
So how can you use this powerful information to your advantage? The solution is simple but fundamental: protect the environment and work for your own good. Here are some important activities that will change your brain through the environment:

Surround yourself with positive and supportive people: build relationships that feed your thoughts and feelings. The people around you have a huge influence on the structure of your brain.

Look for challenges that take you out of your comfort zone: don't be afraid to take on new challenges, learn new things, or take on responsibilities that force you to grow. The brain needs challenges to grow.

Create a stimulating physical environment: Whether at home or at work, make sure your environment is visually stimulating and inspires you to work, learn, and think creatively. Design, color, natural light, and texture can all do wonders for your brain.

Prioritize rest and relaxation: Your brain needs time to rest and regroup. Meditation, proper rest, and contact with nature can help restore brain health.

Act Now: Change Your Environment to Change Your Life
This is not a complete piece of advice. This is a scientific plan that can be applied immediately. Your environment not only influences you, but can be your strongest partner in your personal and professional development. If you want to optimize your brain for success, the first step is to change your environment. Your brain has unlimited potential, it just needs the right environment to do its job.

It's time to take care of your environment. Remember: the brain affects not only what you do, but also how you live your life. Change your environment and you will change your life.

DESIGNING ORGANIZATIONAL CULTURES THAT FAVOR GROWTH

The Key to Sustainable Success

In a changing global economy, growth is not an option, it is a necessity. Here's the truth few people want to hear: The key to long-term success isn't in individual strategies, but in the organizational culture you create. If your organization isn't designed to support growth, it doesn't matter how good your product is or how talented your team is. You can't go too far.

Why is organizational culture the engine that drives growth? Culture is an everyday thing because it is not inscribed in the values of a company. It is the affective, emotional and work environment in which employees communicate, learn, innovate and develop. Your organization's culture is the foundation for the development of creativity, motivation, and success.

Now think about whether you can improve this culture. Imagine if you could create an environment where everyone felt inspired, challenged, and encouraged to reach their potential. This isn't just a dream, it's a scientifically proven fact that you can realize today.

Why is culture more important than ever?
It challenges the idea that companies can grow solely from ideas and visions. Of course, it's important to have a clear vision and a good strategy, but they can't reach their potential without the support of a culture that fosters innovation, learning, and collaboration.

Page 170

Neuroscience teaches us something powerful: the human brain learns, adapts, and grows in the right environment. This applies not only to individuals but also to the collective brain of an organization. When people feel like they're in an environment that values trial, error, and continuous learning, the result is growth for both individuals and organizations.

Research on the development of growth
Did you know that companies that encourage growth and learning have more engaged, creative, and happy employees? This is the neuroscience of collaboration: when you create an environment where people can learn without fear of failure, their brains activate reward-related areas. In other words, they have positive thoughts that encourage motivation and the desire to continue learning and growing.

This is because oxytocin (the "love hormone" or communication hormone) is increased in people in an environment where cooperation is valued. This chemical in the brain promotes cooperation and trust in a team. Conversely, an environment that encourages intense competition or fear of failure will increase the stress hormone cortisol, inhibiting creativity, innovation, and productivity.

5 Tips for Creating an Organizational Culture for Growth
Have you ever wondered how I can transform my organization into a place for regular growth? The answer is clear: start by creating a good culture. Here are 5 tips based on research and experience that you can use right away:

The Mind of a Leader

1. Create a lifelong learning environment
Learning should never stop. Make lifelong learning a priority. Provide regular training, engaging feedback, and opportunities to foster a growth mindset. Employees should feel that they have the opportunity to make mistakes and learn without fear of being judged or failing.

Research supports this idea: when people have the opportunity to make mistakes and learn from them, they feel stronger and therefore become more innovative and active. It's a culture that fosters creativity and excellence.

2. Build collaboration, not competitive teams
It's time to dispel the myth that only "competitors" can achieve great things. The real power of an organization is in the groups that support each other and share knowledge.

Neuroscience confirms it: when people work together, their brains connect better, creating a synergy that would be impossible in a competitive environment. Collaboration unleashes collective creativity and allows each member to contribute their strengths in unique ways.

3. Trust the backbone of your organizational culture
Nothing hinders growth more than doubt. There is no innovation without trust. When people feel they can make an impact without fear of being judged or rejected, psychological damage occurs and the brain opens up to new possibilities.

Promote ethics, openness and respect. Neuroscience shows that a religious environment reduces stress,

Page 172

increases productivity, and fosters a sense of belonging, thereby increasing loyalty and commitment.

4. Consider failure as part of the path to success
If there is no work, there is no growth. Celebrate lessons instead of punishing mistakes. Let failure become the springboard to future success.

When organizations can avoid mistakes, the brain becomes immune to the psychological effects of fear. Employees feel more confident in taking calculated risks that can lead to significant and unprecedented discoveries. The fear of failure is the greatest enemy of success.

5. Improve the overall health of employees
Chronic stress and mental illness are the silent enemies of growth. Without considering the physical and mental health of employees, organizational culture will not reach its potential.

Participation in health services, the provision of flexible working and the creation of a suitable environment for work-life balance are important. Remember, a rested and healthy, creative and collaborative mind is essential.

Act Now: The Way You Need to Grow Is in Your Hands
Imagine an organization where every team member feels supported, valued, and empowered to reach their full potential. Can you see how this culture of growth can transform your company? This is not a long-term vision or a strategic choice; This is the key to continued and widespread success.

The best part: it's at your fingertips. As a leader, you are the creator of your organization's culture. If you act now and start designing a culture that values learning, collaboration, trust, and innovation, you'll be on the most important path to sustainable, never-ending growth.

Don't miss it. The future belongs to those who build an organizational culture based on sustainable growth. Are you ready to start this journey? It's time to make your habit work for you.

James Lass

THE NEUROSCIENCE OF RECOGNITION AND MOTIVATION

The Secret to Unleashing Human Potential

Imagine a world where every member of your team feels energized and their motivation increases simply by recognizing their strengths. What if you knew that this isn't just an emotional touch, but the neurochemicals that could transform your business? Yes, the neuroscience of recognition is so complex that it can make the difference between a normal team and an unstoppable team.

In a workplace where expectations are high and competition is fierce, genuine recognition isn't just a kind gesture – it's the key to unleashing boundless energy on your team. And most importantly: everything is in your hands.

If you think recognition is a fun and beneficial strategy for employees, think again. Acceptance is closely related to motivation and motivation, in turn, is a powerful driver of performance and excellence. Do you want to know how? Here we tell you using the scientific method.

The Power of Persuasion: The Science Behind Motivation
Human motivation is driven by complex brain systems, but the reward system is key. When we meet someone, the brain releases important chemicals like dopamine and oxytocin. These neurotransmitters, called hormones, directly affect our emotions. Dopamine motivates us to keep acting because it gives us pleasure and satisfaction.

The Mind of a Leader

Again, oxytocin makes us feel connected and part of a group.

Now think that every time someone on your team makes an effort, you really appreciate it. Recognition activates certain parts of the brain that are activated by reward or physical reward. This will not only improve their current attitude, but will also increase their willingness to continue participating. The brain seeks out more such rewards, creating a cycle of self-reinforcement.

But here's the key: genuine recognition has a more lasting impact than automatic "good job" claims. Personal and personal recognition creates great brain rewards, empowering employees to a level you never imagined.

Why is anonymous persistence not enough?
The human brain is designed to seek rewards. If an employee works overtime or tries too hard to be recognized, their brain doesn't get the recognition it needs. Over time, this can make you feel tired, irritable, and lose energy. Recognition not only provides instant gratification, but it also aligns individual and company goals, creating common goals that strengthen relationships.

What happens when people are not recognized? Not knowing activates the amygdala, the part of the brain associated with fear and anxiety. If these things happen out of control, they can lead to depression, anxiety, and emotional exhaustion that affect your performance.

Page 176

Cognitive Leadership Skills: Direct Material Results

Effective leaders are sensitive to the power of obedience. Neuroscience has shown that leaders who recognize and celebrate their team's accomplishments not only improve morale, but also increase productivity and creativity. A motivated team member feels valued and appreciated by a team whose work is committed to furthering the organization's goals.

Imagine your employees waking up each day with a clear purpose, knowing that their efforts will be noticed, appreciated, and rewarded. Isn't that the best way to increase innovation, productivity, and job satisfaction?

Acceptance is the key that moves the engine
Just saying "thank you" is not enough. To make the most of your team's potential, recognition needs to be accurate, targeted, and timely. Here are neuroscience-based strategies you can put into practice right away:

1. Identify motivation, not results
Motivation depends not only on performance, but also on action. When an employee is recognized for their continued effort, even if the results aren't good, a sense of satisfaction takes over their brain. Acceptance creates a desire to keep improving because the brain associates effort with reward.

2. Be personal and specific
General "good works" do not affect personal approval. Acknowledging a member's special actions not only shows that you care, but it also activates the brain activity associated with genuine appreciation. "I'm really

impressed with how you handled this problem" is more powerful than "good job."

Publicly acknowledging their strengths reinforces the belief that the company values a job well done. However, it's important not to overdo it because when the valuation seems false or exaggerated, it can lose its power.

3. Be Timely: Don't Wait Too Long
The brain responds better to immediate rewards. Immediate recognition after a great effort provides immediate feedback, reinforces the behavior, and increases the likelihood that it will be repeated in the future. Don't wait a week to realize your accomplishments, do it now.

4. Create an environment of continuous confession.
Embed compliance into your organization's culture so that it becomes a daily habit, a behavior that everyone in the organization follows.

Take Action Today: Unlock the Power of Your Talented Team
Don't let your team fail or feel invisible. The power of verification is in your hands. Change the game and make your team an engine of energy, creativity, and productivity by recognizing your team's efforts.

Recognition is the key that unlocks the door to great work. If you want a team that is committed, dedicated, and always focused on quality, start using them today. Don't let your team wait for value and satisfaction. Act now and create a motivating culture that will transform your company!

Page 178

INNOVATION AND CREATIVITY IN LEADERSHIP

The Power of Thinking Outside the Box

Have you ever wondered what separates great leaders from average leaders? The answer lies in creativity and innovation. If you think that innovation is the responsibility of research teams or technical departments, you are wrong. Creativity is not a luxury; This is an important requirement for modern leadership.

In the fast-paced business world, where competition is not only in your city but around the world, technical leadership is not an option – you need to survive, thrive, and stand out. Most importantly, we all have the ability to develop creativity. The key is to understand how the human brain works and how to harness its infinite potential to generate vision, creativity, and success.

This blog is a challenge to common beliefs. If you ever thought that creativity was the stuff of artists, designers, or inventors, you're wrong. Good leadership is a work in progress. Today I want to show you how the science of

The Mind of a Leader

technology can change your path as a leader and help you achieve success.

Creativity: The Hidden Power of Successful Leaders

Did you know that the brain is designed to create? From the moment we are born, our mind is constantly looking for new connections, ideas, and solutions. The real problem is not that we don't produce, but that most leaders don't know how to produce.

When leaders are faced with difficult decisions or uncertain times, technology is a lifeline. The best ideas don't come from fixed, fixed, or predictable sources. Innovation thrives on uncertainty and controlled chaos. The most creative minds are those that know how to deal with ambiguity, that can see opportunities where others see obstacles.

The brain is activated in complex ways when we are faced with problems. The areas of the brain responsible for problem-solving are the same areas that are activated when new ideas are generated. This means that the most difficult moments can be the most artistically rich. Stress seems to foster new ways of solving problems, and in this environment, the brain has no choice but to think outside of its normal bounds.

The Artificial Brain: Beyond the Simple

Neuroscience tells us that the brain is incredibly flexible: its ability to change, change, and create new connections is endlessly amazing. This means that everyone, regardless of position or situation, can train our minds to be more creative.

Page 180

The brain is not a fixed organ. Divergent thinking is activated in the face of a new problem or challenge, and is the process of generating multiple ideas from scratch. This attitude is at the heart of innovation. As a leader, your ability to foster and embrace these types of ideas in your team can set you apart from the rest.

New powers in leadership
Innovation isn't just about good ideas or things; It also means an agile and flexible organizational culture. Smart leaders not only think differently, but they create an environment that invites everyone to engage in critical thinking.

Innovation leaders are creators of new opportunities. Instead of giving predetermined answers, ask powerful questions that will help you see new things. They are leaders who break down mental barriers, challenge their teams to go beyond traditional paths, explore the unknown, and use brainpower to create disruptive ideas.

A Creative Leader's Brain: How Does It Work?
When you lead with passion, you develop an open mind that is closely related to neuroplasticity. Every time you push your limits, whether it's making a tough decision, using a new strategy, or reinventing the wheel, you activate a part of your brain called the prefrontal cortex.

This area of the brain is responsible for planning, making decisions, and solving complex problems. The more you use it, the more powerful it becomes, allowing you to make faster decisions, adapt better to change, and develop a broader perspective.

Three Ways to Unlock Leadership Interests

If you want to change your leadership style and increase your team's effectiveness, it's time to take some serious steps backed by neuroscience. Updates are just a step away!

1. Challenging Conferences: Stepping Out of Your Comfort Zone

Creativity grows when you move away from standard solutions. As a leader, you need to get out of your daily routines and expose your team to new experiences, projects, and tasks that challenge them to think differently. When human thought stops repeating itself, it becomes more intelligent. It is recommended to try, although failure is optional. Errors are artifacts of art.

2. Think about cooperation: Create a space where ideas can flow freely. Fostering cross-sectoral collaboration and constructive debate is essential for the development of transformative ideas. Different teams with different ideas and unstoppable creativity engines.

3. Make failure a stepping stone to success

Creativity requires courage. As a leader, you must change the narrative of failure. Every failed attempt should be seen as a learning opportunity, not something to be ashamed of. The brain learns best when faced with obstacles because it activates areas of the brain associated with resilience and critical thinking. Encourage your team to give it a try, and if the results don't meet your expectations, consider "failure" as a step toward innovation.

Act now: It's time to show off your leadership skills!

Page 182

Innovation and creativity are not the property of a privileged few: we can all develop them. If you want to be the leader your team needs, it's time to act. Stop waiting for things to happen and start creating your future today.

Don't underestimate the power of creative neuroscience. If you can recognize how your brain and your team's brain reacts to new challenges and ideas, you'll be one step ahead of the competition. Innovation isn't just a competitive advantage, it's the change your company needs to stand out in the global marketplace.

It's time to change your leadership! Don't miss the opportunity to unlock the limitless potential of your mind, your team, and your team.

THE RELATIONSHIP BETWEEN NEUROSCIENCE AND CREATIVITY

Unlock your infinite potential!

Creativity is not a puzzle reserved for a few artists or experts. NO Creativity is a skill that we all have. But what many don't know is that behind all creativity there is a complex dance of brain activity that, understood and applied, can transform your personal and professional life.

Today I will challenge you to think differently, to break down the mental barriers that tell you that "you are not creative enough" or "creativity is only in the hands of the chosen ones". Neuroscience tells us otherwise. It tells us that we all have the power to create because the human brain is designed to innovate, combine ideas in unique ways, and most importantly, reprogram itself.

. If you've ever thought that creativity is meaningless, unattainable, or reserved only for "artistic" thinking, it's time to think again. The neuroscience of creativity has opened new doors to understanding how the human brain works during new ideas, new solutions, and most importantly, how we can nurture this creative process. And most importantly: we can all train it.

The Science of the Creative Brain: How Does It Work?
. Creation is not a gift from God. It is a brain skill that can be trained and improved. The human brain has amazing neural capacity, which means it can integrate

Page 184

information and adapt to new ways of thinking throughout its life.

When faced with a problem or the need to find a new solution, several parts of the brain work:

Frontal cortex: It is responsible for making decisions, plans, and thinking clearly. This is the part of the brain that works when you need to think differently, that is, when you need to think of several ideas or solutions to the same problem.

Temporal Lobe: This lobe is important for processing memories and emotions and plays an important role in creativity by allowing the integration of ideas in different areas. The unique relationship between ideas is where new ideas are born.

The limbic system: The emotional brain, a source of motivation. Creativity often arises from the desire, from the feeling of solving something or creating something new. The more emotionally involved you are in a project, the more creative you can become.

The Social Brain: Creativity is also related to our relationships. The human brain is designed to work together. In an environment that encourages collaboration, new ideas can be generated by sharing ideas and creating a safe space for ideas.

The Power of Neuroplasticity: Rediscovering Your Creative Mind
The concept of neuroplasticity is one of the most exciting discoveries in modern neuroscience. It refers to the brain's ability to adapt, adapt, and change patterns

throughout life. This means that regardless of your age or background: you can train your brain to be creative.

Think of your brain as a network of pathways. Every time you have a new idea, a new idea, or a new solution, you create a new emotional path. The more you practice creative thinking, the easier the process will be. In fact, when you encounter a problem or problem, your brain first looks for the network, but if there is not enough communication, the brain creates new ones.

Creativity is not just thinking: it is connecting.

Creativity is not just thinking about something new. It's the ability to make strange connections between seemingly unrelated things. The more you practice making connections, the easier it will be for your brain to develop new ideas.

Neuroscience shows us that creativity flourishes when you're in a state of relaxation or "flow," when you stop thinking and allow your brain to break free from the constraints of linear thinking. This is because when you rest, your brain can access different memories and create new associations. Let your mind wander, explore without limits. Creativity arises when there are no limitations.

Creating Paradise: Solving Problems and Breaking the Rules
The brain needs energy to learn how to make new connections. Unique challenges and experiences open the way to new ways of thinking. This is what creative leaders do all the time: they challenge their comfort zones, break their intellectual rules, and dare to face the unknown.

A dynamic and flexible environment that encourages exploration is a great breeding ground. Scientific research has shown that when a person feels psychologically safe, when they are not afraid of failure, their brain opens up new ways of thinking. Fear and rigidity stifle creativity, but confidence and ingenuity unlock it.

Change Your Creativity: Take Action Now
If you want to unleash your creativity, you need to start today. Neuroscience is clear: creativity is not something we are born with, it is something we develop. What's even more amazing is that your brain responds faster when you practice thinking outside the box.

I invite you to introduce yourself to new things, break down your mental barriers, and let your brain change on its own. Challenge your beliefs about what you can achieve. Ask the hard questions. Research. The most important thing is that you are not afraid to fail. Every mistake is an opportunity to create a new network.

It's time to free yourself from your limitations and open the door to creativity. The human brain is your best friend. Use your infinite creativity and turn every idea into a skill.

TECHNIQUES FOR FOSTERING INNOVATIVE IDEAS IN TEAMS

Unleash Your Team's Creative Power Today!

What if you turned every work meeting into a factory of good ideas, a place where solutions flow easily and imperceptibly? What if you could unlock the secrets within your team and unleash the creativity and collaboration that changed your team's direction?

I will tell you an undeniable fact: innovation is not a gift for a privileged few, but a skill that any group can develop, strengthen, and strengthen. The human brain is designed to create new things, but often the work environment and social dynamics hinder this flow of knowledge. It's time to change this.

Today, I'll show you how to spark creative thinking in your team, challenge shared beliefs, and provide you with neuroscience-backed strategies to unleash the creative potential of everyone on your team. Innovation is not only possible, but necessary for the success and growth of an organization.

Common myths about innovation
First, let's address some common myths that can prevent a team from doing so:

Myth 1: "Innovation is only for experts". It's not about coming up with a brilliant idea out of thin air, it's about being able to make unusual connections, something we're all capable of if we work in the right environment.

Page 188

Myth 2: "Innovation happens automatically." The human brain needs a specific environment to generate new ideas. If you don't know how to create this space, the creative flow will fail.

Myth 3: "The more ideas, the better." Sometimes, a small change in a team member's mindset can open the door to a solution they never thought possible.

The secret to innovation: encouraging the flow of thought Neuroscience has discovered something very powerful: the human brain is highly adaptable. This means that as long as the right conditions are created, they can be trained and modified to develop skills. What to achieve? Below are some brain-science-based strategies that can transform your organization into a sustainable place for innovation.

1. Create an emotionally safe space
The key to unlocking your team's creativity isn't to have a great idea, but to create a safe space where people feel comfortable sharing ideas, even if they seem crazy or scary. When the group is confident, the parts of the brain associated with creative thinking are activated.

Neuroscience tells us that fear of rejection or failure activates the amygdala (the part of the brain that controls fear responses), thereby inhibiting creativity. Conversely, when group members feel supported and accepted, the brain transitions to cognitive freedom. This is something your team should consider without restrictions.

2. Encourage diversity of knowledge
Creativity does not arise from unity of thought, but from diversity of thought. The best teams are those in which

people from different backgrounds, skills, and perspectives come together to solve problems. When you work with people who have different styles and ideas, your brain starts to make strange connections.

Encourage different perspectives. Allow each group member to share their ideas and ask questions that challenge conventional wisdom. Neuroscience says that the brain lights up when you encounter new and different stimuli, the more neural connections there are, which leads to smarter thinking.

Divergent thinking is a process in which the brain creates multiple ways to solve a single problem. Many new ideas arise from the ability to think beyond traditional boundaries. To encourage this type of thinking, it is important to perform exercises that go against the norm.

Tip: Think without judgment.

3: Classic, but with a novelty: instead of checking ideas as they arise, encourage them to make sense. Every idea, no matter how strange, must be respected. The creative brain works best when it doesn't feel judged. Let your thoughts flow without interruption. Then you can slowly download the most promising ones.

Suggested approach: "What if
Ask persuasive questions that open up new possibilities. For example, "What if we don't have a way?", "What if everything we know is wrong?" or "What if this is something completely different?"

4. Incubation: Give the brain time to work

One of the most amazing ways the brain creates new ideas is through the incubation process. This happens when you allow your brain to "rest" from problems and allow thoughts to continue to form in your unconscious mind.

Your brain isn't useless when you don't think deeply about the answers. Instead, it works in the background, processing information and looking for patterns. During this period, neural connections are strengthened and creativity emerges naturally. That's what great leaders do: they give space to think and allow new ideas to emerge, rather than force them.

5. Encourage open and seamless collaboration
Creativity thrives in an open, collaborative environment where ideas flow freely and people aren't afraid to offer their unstructured ideas. The human brain shines when it can share ideas in a collaborative environment.

An effective technique is to use focus groups, where each group complements the other. When information is shared, creative relationships are created. Create an environment where everyone has a voice and ideas are not rejected but adopted.

6. Accept failure as part of the process
Fear of failure is one of the biggest barriers to innovation. The brain must be afraid to connect with new ideas. Easy and convenient, no learning curve required. Allow your team to make mistakes, because every mistake is one more step toward innovation.

What to do: Transform your organization toward innovation

Innovation is not something that only a few can achieve. This is a skill that any team can achieve if the right conditions are created. As a leader, your job is to create an environment that challenges conventional wisdom, welcomes different ideas, celebrates mistakes, and most importantly, empowers your team to think without limits.

It's time to unleash your team's creative potential, challenge what you thought was possible, and change your perspective on what's new. What you do is only the first step and your brain will thank you.

Take action now and start building an unstoppable team of experts!

HOW TO GET OUT OF LIMITING THOUGHT PATTERNS

Unlock your potential now

Have you ever felt stuck in a cycle of thoughts that are holding you back? Thoughts that tell you, "I'm not ready," "It doesn't make sense," or "I can't do it," seem so true, so natural, that we often don't bother them if I tell you. Are they just dumb? You can change them, you can get rid of them and unlock unlimited possibilities for success, happiness, and personal growth.

Page 192

Today I will take you on a journey into your brain. Our goal is to shed light on the secrets of limiting factors, find out how they limit your potential, and give you the scientific and practical tools you need to overcome them. Neuroscience has shown that you can rewire your mind. But you need to know how to do it, and most importantly, you can get started today.

What is mental retardation?
Limiting thoughts are deep-seated beliefs we have about ourselves, others, or the world that tell us what we can and can't do. These ideas are not true, they are a misinterpretation of reality. The problem is not that these thoughts exist, but that without questioning them we continue to act as if they were.

A common example of deductive reasoning is a phrase like:

"I don't know how."
"I always fail, so it's not worth trying."
"This is where I live, I can't change it."
Why are they strong? Because the human brain is programmed to look for coherence, find ways to repeat and validate what it already believes. In short: our brain loves familiarity, even if it holds us back.

The Science Behind Control: Why Are Our Brains So Programmed?
Did you know that neuroscience has shown that mental retardation is based on physical and mental processes in the brain? Everything we think, believe, and experience leaves an imprint on our neurobiology. These processes are called neural connections. Nerve connections are the

thought pathways in the brain. The more a thought is repeated, the stronger the connection.

Emotional processes related to self-criticism or fear of failure, for example, are reinforced every time you think negatively about yourself. It creates well-defined pathways in the brain, making it easier to think about the same thing over and over again. The problem is that these roads become busy over time. Your brain begins to use these shortcuts unconsciously, increasing feelings of inadequacy or fear of failure.
But here's the good thing: your brain is plastic, there's something called neuroplasticity. In short, it means you can change course and create new relationships that promote good ideas, inspire, and empower.

How to Read Minds: Strategies Based on Neuroscience

1. Pay attention and question your thoughts
The first step is to identify these limiting patterns. Stop by and see what you think. What is the automatic thought that comes to mind when you are faced with a problem? What do you say to yourself when you think about a new project or achieve a goal?

Ask the important question: Is this idea true? Science shows that our limiting beliefs are misinterpretations. These are not facts, but assumptions based on fear and past experiences. Asking and questioning these thoughts is like putting some brakes on your amazing path. Do this every day, and you'll find that these thoughts don't have much power over you.

2. Redefine your personal story: from "I can't" to "I can"

It's very important to change the way you talk to yourself. Negative self-talk leads to diminished style. Research in neuroscience shows that internal stories play an important role in how we perceive our abilities and potential. If you keep telling yourself that you can't do it, your brain starts to think it's true.

The key is to replace these thoughts with something positive and achievable. It's not about creating something that isn't true, but about focusing on your strengths and what you've achieved so far. Write your story. Instead of thinking, "I can't do it," you can start with something like, "I've overcome problems before and I know I can do it again."

3. Practice meditation and meditation
Meditation and meditation are powerful tools for removing limiting thoughts. Science proves it: meditation activates the prefrontal cortex, the area of the brain responsible for rational thinking and self-control. This will help you break the cycle of negative thoughts and take the step of looking at them without judgment.

In practice, meditation teaches you to be more aware of your thoughts and to decide what you need to know. If a limiting thought arises, instead of letting it control you, you can let it go and choose a better thought. .
not bad. Gratitude is one of the best ways to achieve this.

Practice gratitude every day. Recognize your accomplishments, no matter how small. This helps the brain's reward cycle, releasing dopamine, a neurotransmitter that produces motivation and a sense of well-being. When you focus on your success, you're developing new strategies that will help you meet future challenges with confidence.

4. Stick to it: adjust your thinking through repetition
The key to changing your weight loss habits is perseverance. When you use these techniques, it will be easier to develop new habits of mind. Don't look for instant results, but if you don't change, you'll see the beginning of new neural connections in the old places.

Remember, neuroplasticity means you can rewire your brain. It's hard work, patience, and perseverance.

It's time to act!
Now that you know how to get rid of negative thoughts, it's time to put what you've learned into practice. Break the chains that hold you back, connect with your brain, and release the infinite potential waiting to be unleashed.

This is not an option, you leave tomorrow. Every day is great. Every thought you change, every action you take to challenge your limiting beliefs, is a way to change. Don't let fear, doubt, or insecurity rule you again.

Act now! Start taking control of your thoughts today and see the difference it will make in your life!

Page 196

James Lass

PRACTICAL TOOLS FOR THE NEUROCONSCIOUS LEADER

Conquer your mind, conquer your team

Many leaders think that in order to be successful, they must rely on their skills, years of experience, or even their passion. But today I want to challenge you to think differently. True leadership is not in what you know how to do, but in how you know how to lead your heart and that of your team. This is what characterizes a neuroconscious leader: someone who understands the power of their brain and uses this knowledge to make smarter decisions, connect with their team, and lead them.

Can you get out of the traditional culture and have a positive outlook? If so, this blog is for you.

Today I'm going to introduce you to a useful tool based on neuroscience research that can change the way you lead and change the way your entire team works. It's time to improve your chances and learn how to be a leader that everyone admires and follows. And best of all, you can get started now.

What is a rational leader?
Before we dive into the tools, it's important to understand what it means to be an effective leader. A neuroscience leader is not just someone who has knowledge about the human brain, but knows how brain structures affect

decision-making, motivation and personal relationships, and organizational performance.

Neuroconscious guidance uses the principles of neuroscience:

Manage stress effectively.

Make a wise decision in your heart.
Boost your team's creativity and growth.
Create organizational cultures that promote collaboration and well-being.
Build relationships with all team members.
This approach will not only improve your performance as a leader, but it will transform the workplace, increase productivity, motivate, and retain talent.

Tools to help the professional leader
Now that you know what a smart leader is, let's explore some research tools and techniques you can start using today to take your leadership to the next level.

1. Immunity: the key to decision-making
In a distracted world, the ability to control your thoughts is critical. Studies have shown that mindfulness activates the area of the brain responsible for rational decision-making. A neuroconscious leader understands that their mind is their greatest asset, so they learn to focus on what's important.

How to get there? Practice mindfulness or listening with mindfulness. The simple process of not focusing on the present allows you to understand past events and make decisions based on information rather than emotions. Meditation improves the function of the prefrontal cortex, the center of thinking and decision-making. By training your mind to be present, you develop your ability to make quick and accurate decisions even in times of crisis.

2. *Neuroplasticity*: Reprogramming Your Brain for Success Did you know that you can retrain your mind to become a better leader? If, instead of repeating such limited thoughts, you decide to create a new brain that wants to lead, the change will be beneficial.

How are you? Challenge the limits of your beliefs. If you think "I'm not a good leader" or "I'm not creative," change that statement. Start focusing on your successes, no matter how small, and celebrate each step toward your progress. The repetition of positive and positive thoughts increases the brain's ability to relate to success, motivation, and self-confidence. Through repetition, new neural pathways are strengthened and eventually become a new way of thinking.

3. And research backs it up: When you show empathy, you open up parts of the brain that directly affect emotions, trust, and connection. A neuroconscious leader understands that collaboration is essential for productivity and value.

How to use it? Start by listening carefully to your team. Not only to hear their words, but also to understand their desires. Use open-ended questions and give people space to express their opinions. Make eye contact, use supportive gestures, and show appreciation for your challenges and successes. This creates a safe and collaborative environment where people want to share their ideas and concerns.

4. Manage stress: Stay calm

Stress is one of the biggest enemies of good decision-making. A neuroconscious leader knows that stress directly affects their brain and limits their ability to think clearly and make the right decisions. But you also know that stress is inevitable. The most important thing is to learn to control it.

How to get there? Take deep breaths when you feel anxiety increase. Deep breathing activates the parasympathetic system, which is responsible for calming the body and reducing stress. Breathe in 4-7-8, inhale for 4 seconds, hold your breath for 7 seconds, and exhale slowly for 8 seconds. This simple exercise can reduce the activity of the amygdala, the part of the brain responsible for emotional reactions. make the most appropriate decisions.

5. Positive feedback: Encourage positive behavior

Positive feedback is an effective tool for improving your team's motivation and performance. Neuroscience has shown that positive reinforcement activates the brain's reward centers and releases dopamine, the neurotransmitter of pleasure and motivation.

How to implement? Be sure to give quick and specific feedback. Appreciate your team's work, not just the end. By doing this, you'll reinforce positive feedback and increase productivity, creativity, and engagement.

Are you ready to be the neuroconscious leader your team needs?

Becoming a neuroconscious leader isn't just a trend, it's a revolution in leadership. Do you dare to challenge the status quo and use your brainpower to achieve unexpected results?

Time to work. Start implementing these tools today and see how your team responds. Self-awareness, compassion, and emotional control will not only transform your leadership, but also your organization's environment and culture.

Remember: change starts with you. Don't wait too long. Everyone's favorite Neuroconscious guide is waiting to be published. It's your time to shine!

EXERCISES TO IMPROVE DECISION MAKING

Challenge Your Mind and Transform Your Leadership!

Have you ever felt trapped in a sea of decisions? Things that carry a lot of weight, things that can change the course of your life, career, or business. If you've ever wondered if there's a way to make decisions with greater clarity, confidence, and accuracy, this blog is for you.

Decision-making is not just a logical process, it is a skill that can be learned. And best of all, you don't have to be an expert to fix it. All you need is to understand how your brain works and use some practical exercises that will help you make smarter and more effective decisions.

Consider this: you're facing an important decision. Stress overwhelms you, options multiply and the fear of making a mistake paralyzes you. You may not know that your brain is designed to make effective decisions, but you may not be using it to its full potential. I invite you to change your attitude, reorganize your thoughts by making a decision. Science holds the key. Come on, take it!

Why is decision-making important?
Decision-making is one of the most complex and important processes in our lives. From the simplest day-to-day decisions to important decisions that can determine the future of your career or company, everything is based on brain processes. Fortunately, our brains are plastic, which means we can practice and improve.

Neuroscience shows that several factors influence our decisions: emotions, stress, limiting beliefs, and external pressures. However, by training your brain and doing some mental exercises, you'll be able to make faster, more efficient decisions that align with your goals.

Exercise No. 1: Options Analysis Using the "Rule of Three Circles"
Have you ever felt like you have too many options and don't know where to start? This exercise is perfect for removing clutter and allowing your brain to focus on what's really important.

How to do it:

Draw three circles on a piece of paper.
In the first circle, write down all the possibilities you have, even the most dangerous or unexpected ones.
In the second circle, write down what's important to you in this decision (e.g., your values, your long-term goals, your team's well-being).
In the third circle, write down the short- and long-term consequences of each choice.
The three-circle method helps your brain analyze information in an organized and clear way. This exercise makes decisions more real and allows you to see more clearly the impact of each choice. When you align your decisions with your values and goals, doubts are greatly reduced.

Exercise No. 2: The "10-10-10 Model" for Reducing Stress and Anxiety
Stress is one of the biggest enemies of effective decision-making. This clouds our judgment, triggers emotional reactions, and leads us to make quick decisions. The

10-10-10 model, created by author Suzy Welch, is a simple and effective exercise that will help you put difficult decisions into perspective.

How to do it:

First, think about how you'll feel about the decision you'll make in 10 minutes. Will it be a sense of peace? Because of stress? Repent?
Second, think about how you'll feel 10 months from now. Does this decision still have the same impact? How do you get used to it?
Finally, look at how you'll feel 10 years from now. Will you regret this decision? Would you be proud of what you did?
This exercise allows you to see decisions from a different perspective and helps reduce fear of impulse. By giving your brain time to process the impact of a decision at different time intervals, you'll be able to make more informed and rational decisions.

Exercise No. 3: "Decision Journal" for clarification and reflection
Do you feel overwhelmed by the constant decisions you have to make? Decision writing is a powerful tool that trains your brain to think and learn from every choice.

How to do it:

Take 5 to 10 minutes each day to write down important decisions you've made in your journal. It could be something big, like changing jobs, or something small, like changing service providers.

Write down what factors influenced your decision, how you felt when you made the decision, and what you learned from the process.

At the end of each week, review the decisions you wrote down. Do you see any patterns? Which decisions are easier to make and which are harder? What strategy did you use to make this decision?

This exercise has two effects: not only will it help you train your mind to make clearer decisions, but it will also allow you to learn from each experience and improve your decision-making process over time.

Exercise No. 4: "Advanced Decision-Making Techniques" to Boost Your Confidence

When you make decisions under pressure, your brain easily becomes stressed and doubtful. This exercise will allow you to practice making quick and confident decisions without the paralyzing fear of making mistakes.

How to do it:

Create a scale from 1 to 10, where 1 is a low-impact decision (e.g., choosing lunch) and 10 is a high-impact decision (e.g., accepting a job).

Practice quick decisions in everyday situations where risk is minimal. For example, what movie should we watch tonight? Which book to read? Which projects should you start first?

As you move up the ladder, try to make decisions faster without thinking too much about the consequences. This way you will practice self-confidence and mental dexterity.

This exercise will help you better manage uncertainty and trust your intuition when making more impactful decisions.

Exercise #5: The "Show Options" Method for Advanced Forecasting

Forecasting is not for elite athletes or dynamic traders — it is a powerful tool that the brain uses to think about various future scenarios and prepare for the future.

How to do it:

If you're faced with an important decision, close your eyes and imagine your life after you make each decision.
Ask yourself: How will I feel about this decision in the future? How will it change my life and my life?
It should now be done multiple times with different options and options. This helps the brain make mental predictions about the outcome.
Visualization can reduce stress, increase clarity, and help you make decisions that affect your life.

It's time to change your mind!
Not only are the most successful leaders able to make decisions quickly, but they also have intelligence, confidence, and a deep understanding of the brain that influences their decisions. It's not just luck: it's training your brain to make smart decisions that align with your goals.
Break your old habits, wash away the chains of ignorance, and start using this game today. Decision-making is a skill that can be developed and the sooner you start, the sooner you will see amazing results.

Remember, the most important decision you can make here is action. The future awaits you and your mind, trained to make the right decisions, will be your best friend along the way.

Page 206

James Lass

It's time to govern!

TECHNIQUES TO TRAIN EMPATHY AND EMOTIONAL REGULATION

Transform Your Leadership and Your Life

How to Develop Patience and Emotional Control: Change Your Life and Life
In today's fast-paced business world, quick decisions and bold plans are important, but so is the ability to connect with people n, of course. This is not just "soft" art. It is the key to success, in your personal and professional life. But it's something you can buy. Science backs it up: empathy and emotion regulation are skills that can be developed.
. Or are you able, in times of intense pressure, to communicate effectively or make decisions without the burden of emotions? If you've experienced this, you know that it's important to know these skills.

You may not know that your brain is great at changing and improving in these areas, but you can train it in scientifically proven ways to improve it, not your government, but it will change your life.

It's time to challenge deeply held beliefs about emotions. It's not an obstacle, it's an advantage. It is not something that should be controlled, it is something that can be trained. So today we will show you how.

Why is it important to practice empathy and emotional management?
Emotions are just a response to what happens to us. It is an inner compass that shows us what we want and what

we fear, but if we do not know how to use it correctly it will remain silent.

Compassion is, more importantly, the ability to put yourself in another person's shoes, understand their feelings, and respond appropriately. This is important as a leader, because connecting emotionally with your team, your customers, or yourself allows you to build better relationships, increase trust, and strengthen collaboration.

The law of emotions, however, is not about restricting our thoughts, but about directly directing those emotions. Emotions are powerful and when we manage them well, they force us to make informed decisions.

The power of these two abilities individually cannot be stopped. The good news is that you can train and take care of it. Below are some practical ways to be more compassionate, honest, and productive.

Technique No. 1: "Active Listening and Passive Response"
One of the biggest barriers to empathy is listening carefully. In our daily struggles, we often hear the answer rather than understand it. Compassion begins when we truly listen to others, not just their words, but their deepest feelings.

How to do it:

Listen and don't talk. Let the other person have their say.
Keep an eye on body language, gestures, and tone of voice. Many times what is not said is as important as what is said.

After listening, think about your feelings. Use phrases like "I see you're worried about this" or "I know you're worried about this."

Ask open-ended, thoughtful questions, such as, "What do you think about this?" or "What would you like to change?"

This activity will help you get to know the feelings of others and strengthen your empathy skills. And not only that, it creates a climate of trust in your team, which translates directly into productivity and collaboration.

Strategy #2: "Mental changes for emotional management"

Emotions do not appear for no reason. Our event descriptions are descriptions that evoke emotions. The emotional process begins by changing the way we interpret and react to situations. This is where cognitive restructuring comes in, a process based on emotional intelligence that allows you to change your emotional reactions to difficult situations.

How to do it:

Identify the negative thoughts that are causing the feeling (e.g., "This is an accident, I can't fix it").

Question the soundness of the idea. Is that bad? Is there any evidence that this is true?

Replace it with positive thoughts: "This is challenging, but I have the skills to do it" or "I can learn something important from this experience."

Look deeply, calm down. It may only be a few seconds, but those seconds make all the difference. The exercise It will train you to control your emotions, allowing you to do better and calmer, even in stressful situations.

Technique #3: "Psychological Analysis Technique"
Critical thinking is one of the most powerful tools you can use to control your emotions and make decisions. When we are stressed, angry, or sad, we react quickly. Parents are resting. Instead of being happy, take some time to connect with yourself.

How to do it:

Before responding to an emotional situation, pause for three seconds (or longer if necessary). Take a deep breath.
Connect with your feelings: What are true feelings? Why do you do that?
Consider: How can you resolve this situation? What is important to you in the end? Norm
about choice and discretion. Respond in a calm, positive, and loving manner.
This simple practice will allow you to make the right decisions and avoid impulsive reactions that can harm your superiors.

Technique #4: "Compassion"
If you want to develop deep and lasting compassion, there is no better practice than compassion meditation. This technique, called "Metta", helps you connect with the lives of others, while working on your inner peace.

How to do it:

Sit in a quiet place and close your eyes.
Start by thinking about someone close to you (friend, colleague) and repeat in your mind: "May everything go well for you, may you be happy, may you be at peace and

happiness." your life to other people, even those who are not close to you. Focus on wishing them well.
Open your heart to these people and sympathize with their good life.
Not only does compassionate meditation increase your compassion for others, but it also reduces stress, improves your mood, and improves your leadership skills by promoting a positive and open mind.

It's time to act!
Today's world needs leaders who are not only wise and intelligent, but also intellectual. Compassion and emotional control are more than just additional skills; It is important to create a work environment, improve decision-making and develop trusting and lasting relationships.

So why wait? Science is on your side: you can train your brain to be compassionate, control your emotions, and ultimately become an effective, balanced, and compassionate leader.

It's time to start practicing! Your future as a leader depends on how you train your mind today.

GUIDE TO INCORPORATING NEUROLEADERSHIP INTO EVERYDAY LIFE

Transform Your Leadership and Your Mind

In the competitive and fast-paced world we live in, we must not only enjoy what we do, but also be unique. The leaders of the future aren't just smart people, but people who understand how their brains work and how to use it to lead effectively. This is where neuroleadership comes in, a discipline that changes not only the way we lead others, but also the way we lead ourselves.

What if I told you that the secret to leadership change isn't old management policies or quick decisions? What if I told you about how your brain reacts to stress, stimuli, emotions, and relationships? Neuroleadership holds the key to unlocking unlimited potential within you and the people you lead.

The good news is that it's not just for neuroscientists, you can incorporate neuroleadership into your daily life in meaningful and effective ways. And I promise you that the change will be profound!

What is Neurotrend and why does it affect you?
Neuroleadership is a science that combines neuroscience and leadership to improve the way we lead. This study focuses on understanding how the human brain reacts to leadership situations, how we make decisions, manage our emotions, and how we interact with others.

The Mind of a Leader

The great thing about neuroscience is that it not only helps us understand other people's brains, but it also gives us the power to change our own. From decision-making and stress management to the development of emotional intelligence, neuroleadership provides us with scientifically proven tools to improve our performance and well-being.

Incorporating neuroleadership into everyday life: a change of mindset
To incorporate neuroleadership into everyday life, you don't need to make sudden changes. You should only start with small changes, things that affect your thoughts, make decisions, and connect with others. Here are some of the most powerful keys to incorporating neuroleadership into your daily life:

1. Changing the Way We Make Decisions: Action with Purpose
Decision-making is one of the pillars of neuroleadership. Our brains are used to making quick decisions, but not always the right ones. Emotions and rational thinking lead to hasty decisions, without considering all possible options and consequences.

Solution: To apply neuroleadership, take a break before making big decisions. Ask:

Am I making decisions based on my feelings or my objective data?
Have I considered all possible ideas?
How will this decision affect my members or stakeholders?
This relaxation effectively allows your brain to work from a calm, rational state rather than rushing. This

simple change can make the difference between a reactive decision and a revolutionary one.

2. Stress management: you're not a machine, you're a human being

Stress is a constant in the life of every leader. Job requirements, expectations, decisions... All of these things can lead to a lot of stress and, if not used properly, affect our health and professional relationships.

Here the neuroscientist gives a very different opinion: stress is not something that should be avoided at all costs, but you have to learn to manage it. The human brain, when stressed, responds with a series of physiological reactions. However, if you train, you can change your stress response and use it to improve energy.

A "good stress" technique can be applied to train the brain to see stress as an opportunity for success rather than anger.

Try this:

When you feel stress rising, take a deep breath to activate your parasympathetic nervous system (which allows you to relax).
Change your focus: Instead of thinking "I can't do this," think "this challenge is preparing me to do it."
Use stress as a sign that your brain is working at its maximum capacity.

3. Connect and motivate your team: use the science of emotion

Motivation and emotional connections are fundamental to neuroleadership. The human brain is designed to make emotional connections, and those connections play an important role in how people function as a group.

If you want a high-performing team, you need to think about everyone and understand them. But it is not enough to be a good communicator. It is necessary to understand how the brain reacts to stimuli.

The "good reward" principle is important here: When your partner does a good job, you know that the dopamine system works directly in their brain, which motivates them to do good.

Don't forget that to make your team happy it is also important to help them control their emotions. Compassionate leaders are those who understand emotions, not only their own, but those of others, and act accordingly.

4. Growth Thinking: Not Just for You, But Your Team
The main goal of neuroleadership is growth thinking. This philosophy is based on the idea that our abilities, knowledge, and capabilities are not fixed, but can be developed through effort and learning.

To apply this to your daily life, start acting like a leader. Do you have a challenge? Instead of thinking, "I can't do this," think, "How can I learn from this to improve?" Then share this idea with your team.

By encouraging people to see their weaknesses during learning opportunities, parts of neural plasticity in their brains are activated, helping them overcome conflicts and continue to grow.

The Future as Neuroconscious Leaders: Act Now

Neuroleadership is not just action, it is reflection. This neuroscience-based approach will not only improve your performance, but also make you more humane, smarter, and more efficient.

Today is a great time to start incorporating these principles into your daily life. Science can help you. The benefits are not illusory, they are immediately visible and tangible. Neuroconscious leadership allows you to lead with intuition, clarity, and compassion, make decisions, manage stress effectively, and connect deeply with your team.

Are you ready to change the future of leadership? The power is in your brain and you can train it now! Take the first step in neuroleadership today and start transforming your life and your results as a leader.

THE FUTURE OF TRANSFORMATIONAL LEADERSHIP

The Revolution You're Ignoring

Have you ever thought that traditional leadership is obsolete? If so, be honest. The future of cultural change is not just a trend, it is a brain revolution that is changing now and will change the way we understand leadership for years to come!

Transformational leadership, which is now more focused on motivating, empowering, and changing the people you lead, is evolving. It is not enough to have an inspiring leader who promotes the message. Future leadership changes will be based on science, neuroscience, and a deeper understanding of how the human brain works.

But there is something more important: this new culture means not only changing others, but also changing oneself. Are you ready for a change that will take you from an ordinary boss to an extraordinary leader?

The New Era of Leadership: From Inspiration to Change Tomorrow's transformational leaders will not only inspire, but change their beliefs, their team's behaviors, and most importantly, their way of thinking. He is a leader who understands how the human brain processes information, how it makes decisions, and how it connects emotionally with other people.

This new leadership is based on three principles:

Applied neuroscience: Future leaders don't just run people, they control the brain. We now know, thanks to neuroscience, that the human brain is not very resilient (what is known as neuroplasticity). The next change leader will use this knowledge to recreate the thoughts, beliefs, and emotions in their organization so that people not only work better, but also change internally.

Empathy and solidarity: The future of leadership does not depend only on power or authority, but on real feelings. Research shows that when leaders interact with their teams, collaborative processes are created to increase collaboration, trust, and productivity. A leader who understands people's brains, emotions, and motivations has the ability to change an organization's culture to be more positive and dynamic.

Focus on comfort: Future transformational leaders are focused on creating a safe mental environment where partners can take risks, make mistakes, and learn without fear. By understanding how stress affects the brain and how emotional management is essential for high performance, managers can take care of their team's health, foster work and personal development.

Why is the method needed today?
We live in a world that is changing faster than ever. Technology is developing rapidly, job expectations are rising, and uncertainty is constant. With all this, organizations cannot continue with archaic management systems.

The Mind of a Leader

Traditional leadership that focuses solely on status, control, and intelligence doesn't work. The human brain does not respond in the same way to a leadership style based on fear or controlled emotions. We need leaders who know how to motivate people on a deep level, who connect on an emotional level, and who, above all, understand how neuroplasticity can be used to support continuous lifelong learning.

This change is urgent. The next wave of leadership will not be leaders who give orders. Judged by neurocognitive leaders, people who understand how the human brain responds to emotions, stress, motivation, and most importantly, relationships.

Change Your Leaders Now: What Should You Do?
If you want to be part of this change, it's not enough to read about it or learn about the latest scientific research. You have to do it now. Here are some steps you can take now to transform into the neuroconscious leader your organization needs:

Develop your awareness: Before leading others, it is very important to be yourself. Consider how your brain responds to stress, anxiety, and conflict. Think about yourself every day. How do you feel now? How do they affect your decision?

Maintain empathy: Listening is the key to building trust. Don't listen to your team's words, understand their thoughts and feelings. The leaders of the future are not those who have all the answers, but those who know how to ask good questions and connect with people.

Developing neuroplasticity in your team: Helping your team change the boundaries of thinking. Encourage people to step out of their comfort zone. Remember: the brain is indestructible. Encouraging continuous learning, experimentation, and creativity allows the mind to grow and adapt to the challenges it faces.

Maintaining emotional strength is important: Future transformational leaders understand that stress is not only negative, but also an opportunity for growth. Help your team improve morale. Resilience is not overcoming problems, but learning and growing from them.

Improve well-being: use strategies to reduce work stress and improve mental health. Create an environment where your team can feel safe and free to innovate, take risks, and share ideas without fear of judgment.

Your future as a change leader starts today
The future of change leadership is not a luxury or a passing moment: it is an urgent need. If you don't adapt to this new approach based on neuroscience, empathy, and neuroplasticity, you'll be left behind in a world where culture has completely influenced the way we understand and change the human brain.

Don't wait too long! Change starts today. Diving into the future of transformational leadership can change the way you manage your life, your team, and your organization. You're one step closer to becoming the leader the world needs.

Act now to transform your leadership and take your team to new levels of success and prosperity.

The Mind of a Leader

Page 222

HOW NEUROLEADERSHIP REDEFINES SUCCESS

The Mental Revolution You've Been Waiting For

The concept of success is related to the visual story: sales, products, efforts, and achievements. However, the future of success is not what you see. What really changes is the way you think, feel, and relate to others. This is where neuroleadership comes into play. If you've ever thought that success is about achieving external goals, get ready to see that the real revolution is happening inside your brain.

Restoring success: beyond the numbers
Challenges of being a European challenge with deep-seated beliefs about what success is. It's no longer just about climbing the corporate ladder or accumulating achievements. In fact, long-term success is based on a deep understanding of how the human brain works in the areas of leadership, decision-making, motivation, and interpersonal relationships.

Instead of controlling people from the outside, neuroleadership teaches you to lead from within. This change defines what a leader is. It's not just about doing the job right, it's about using the full potential of your brain and your team to make a profound impact.

Neuroleadership: The secret of future leaders
Imagine a leader who understands how the brain works in stressful situations, how to innovate in their team, or how to use neuroplasticity to support continuous improvement. This is the leader of the future. And if

you're wondering how to become one, the answer is clear: neuroleadership.

Neuroleadership is not just a theory, but a discipline that applies the principles of neuroscience to leadership. It helps you understand human behavior at a deeper level and use that knowledge to make better decisions, create more dynamic teams, and develop lasting relationships. Neuroleadership does not change the way we lead, it changes everything.

Why is behavior interpreted as success?
Improves decision-making: Neuroleadership helps you understand how the brain makes decisions, especially in situations. Anxiety and uncertainty activate parts of the brain that cause us to make irrational or irrational decisions. Leaders who practice neuroleadership know how to calm the brain to make good, rational decisions. This understanding can change the way you solve complex problems, reducing the chance of making costly mistakes.

Create internal motivation: Neuroleadership skills are not based on external incentives such as bonuses or overtime rewards. Instead, it focuses on motivating workers. When your team's brain comes from within, engagement, creativity, and productivity increase dramatically. It's a great change in attitude that motivates people not only to work toward a goal, but also to feel an emotional connection to the message.
Improved interpersonal relationships: Transformational leadership based on neuroleadership that focuses on authentic emotions. Scientific research has shown that the human brain is more receptive to empathy and emotional connection. A leader who understands this

knows how to create cross-functional teams and how to build trusting relationships that produce lasting results.

Improved resilience and persistence: Neuroleadership provides insights into how the brain adapts to learning. While stress can be bad, it can also be a growth tool if you know how to cope. Leaders who apply neuroleadership principles can turn adversity into opportunities for learning and growth, building resilience not only for themselves but also for their teams. 44 44 It's not just about external goals, it's about your own growth and impact on others.

This method helps you break out of patterns that have been in place for years, change your beliefs about what you can achieve, and create a growth mindset. By incorporating neuroleadership strategies, you not only develop as a leader, but you become a more complete version of yourself.

Neuroleadership: how to transform your success
The world is changing rapidly, and success is no longer a goal to be achieved. It is a continuous process of growth, adaptation, and learning. Neuroleadership gives you the tools to not only stand your ground, but also to transform your life, your work, and your environment. It makes you step out of your beliefs and realize that you are a leader. It leads you to think and do things that can change the future.

Your Challenge: Be Tomorrow's Leader Today
No more excuses. The future of success is here and depends on thoughtful leadership, brainstorming, and continuous improvement. If you want to be part of the neuroleadership revolution, you need to act now. You

can't wait for change to come. Neuroleadership is the key to unlocking your full potential and changing the way you feel about success.

Now is the time to take the first step towards real change. Stop following the old rules of success and start creating a leadership style based on reality. The future of leadership is here. And you can be a leader who makes a difference.

It's time to lead in a whole new way!

THE NEXT STEPS TO LEAD WITH PURPOSE AND AWARENESS

Awaken the Leader the World Needs

We live in a time of great change. Government as we know it has been abandoned and the future looks completely different. Being guided by purpose and awareness is not a choice, it is an imperative! If you are a leader or aspire to be one, now is the time to leave your old system and enter a new realm where your purpose and consciousness will guide your decisions, relationships, and every plan.

Now is the time to take the next step towards leadership that inspires, transforms, and transforms. But how do you achieve this in a world full of uncertainty, expectations and unprecedented challenges?

In this blog, I invite you to learn how leading with purpose and awareness is not only a way to achieve lasting success, but also a way to increase your personal, professional, and social impact. I challenge you to break down your mental barriers, make decisions, and become the visionary leader our world needs. Best of all, it's easier than you think, but only if you're willing to take the first step.

Why is decisive leadership the future?
Today, many leaders still work from the paradise of the past: quick results, power over people, control, and low profit margins. But here's the hard truth: the model is broken. According to this research, leadership based

solely on material goals and objective results creates an organization without personality.

A leader's true power comes from their ability to lead with purpose: with a clear vision of what they want to achieve, but also with a deep understanding of why they do it. This type of leadership goes beyond business goals and reaches the deepest parts of humanity: emotional connections, positive impact on people's lives, and collective well-being.

The Incredible Benefits of Using Intention and Awareness
Build lasting trust and security. They no longer work for money, but for something that gives them a purpose. Shared goals improve engagement, loyalty, and productivity. Emotional intelligence aligns your decisions with the collective good by creating an environment of trust that impacts at all levels.

Innovation and creativity
Smart and determined leaders create an environment where creativity and innovation can flourish. Conscientiousness and openness to new ideas inspire creativity and allow your team to find solutions without fear of failure. Not only does this type of leadership make you more agile, but it also allows your team to think outside the box, find new ways to solve problems, and create revolutionary products and services.

Improve decision-making
When you're guided by your goals, you think more clearly and focusedly. Decision-making becomes a

thoughtful and informed process that is aligned with your values and long-term goals. Instead of thinking without thinking or giving in to pressure, you can consciously analyze each situation and ensure that every action aligns with your vision and values.

Improve team well-being
Leadership is not only important for results, but also for the well-being of the entire team. Determined leaders promote mental and emotional health by creating an environment that values work-life balance. Science shows that a positive work environment not only increases productivity but also reduces stress, turnover, and job satisfaction.

You change organizational culture
Organizations with smart, purposeful leadership can build sustainable organizational cultures. A company is not only defined by its products or services, but also by the way it treats people. When leaders lead with a clear purpose and act consciously, companies become places of growth, inclusion, and trust, where people feel part of something bigger than themselves.

Next Steps to Becoming a Visionary and Determined Leader If you feel like your leader knows what's coming, but you don't know where to start, here's the first step to changing your leadership style:

Connect with your personal and professional goals
Have a purpose, the "why" behind everything you do. Think carefully about what really inspires you, motivates you, and what you want to leave as a legacy. Make it your own project. Once you are clear on your goals,

share them with your team and make them part of a shared vision.

Mindfulness
Mindfulness is a powerful tool for staying focused, reducing stress, and making clear, informed decisions. Take a few minutes each day to meditate, take deep breaths, and reflect on your mental state and emotions. Mindfulness allows you to calm your mind and focus on the present moment, which is essential to make more effective decisions.

Develop empathy and emotional intelligence
Determined leaders focus on people, not just results. Develop empathy and better understand your team's needs, feelings, and concerns. Listen carefully, value differences, and create an environment of trust. Emotional intelligence helps you communicate effectively with your partners and make decisions that benefit everyone.

Cultivate a Culture of Understanding and Appreciation
As a leader, your actions are an example to others. Be clear about your goals, objectives, and challenges. Appreciate and genuinely recognize your team's work and achievements. This type of leadership creates an environment where people feel valued, thus increasing their engagement and productivity.

Seeking innovation at the service of goals
It is not enough to have goals; You have to find a new way to do it. Encourage team creativity, create an environment of continuous learning, and celebrate disruptive ideas. Constant change and innovation are key

to moving your business forward and maintaining a lasting impact.

It's time to act: the world needs wise men
Now that you understand the power of living through intention and awareness, the other way is clear: it's time to act. You have to change yourself, not wait for the situation to change. The future belongs to leaders who not only know how to achieve personal success, but also strive to make a positive impact and change on people and organizations.

Your turn. The world needs leaders like you. Are you ready to take the next step and define the management of tomorrow?

FINAL INSPIRATION

The Impact of Neuroconscious Leadership on the World

Imagine a world where leaders not only get results, but also have common sense and integrity in all their decisions. A world where companies succeed not because of their profits, but because of the impact they have on people and the world. A world full of understanding, knowledge, and purpose is the engine of progress. Does that sound familiar? It is not like that. This future is just around the corner and you can be the leader who leads it.

Neurocognitive leadership is the key to changing your organization and even the entire world. And now more than ever, the world needs leaders who dare to question the norm, challenge conventional wisdom, and embrace approaches based on neuroscience, logic, and truth.

This is a call to you, who are leaders or want to be, to you who want to leave something deep and beautiful. It is time to take leadership steps that not only think about the future of the company, but also about that of people.

Leadership Neuroscience: The Gaming Revolution
Neuroscience reveals some changes: Our brains aren't designed to function under chronic stress, extreme stress, or toxic work conditions. On the contrary, our brain thrives when it is in an environment that promotes health, connection, and trust.

And how to do this? From a neurocognitive perspective, a leadership that combines the science of the human brain with a deep understanding of human emotions, feelings, and relationships. Neurological leadership is more than just control; It's about knowing and mastering the brain's energy that affects performance, creativity, decision-making, and most importantly, health.

By applying the principles of neuroscience to management, you empower your team to achieve goals and grow. Research shows that when we lead by knowing how the human brain works, we improve development, motivation, and support in our groups. This is not strict or traditional; He is flexible, compassionate, and caring.

Difficulty believing: leadership, not management
For many years we have been invaded by the idea that good leadership depends on the ability to make quick decisions, manage and keep power in the hands of a few. But this product doesn't work. Neuroscience tells us that stress, intense competition, and mental stress inhibit intelligence, reduce creativity, and ultimately weaken organizations.

Neuro Leadership, on the other hand, challenges traditional beliefs. True leadership has no power; It's about making a good impression. When you lead from consciousness, you understand that people want to be valued, heard, and appreciated. Conscious leaders are those who create a mindset where collaboration is the norm and innovation is the norm.

Neuroconscious Leadership Transformation
By using this method, you not only change the way you lead, but you also change the people around you. Here are the surprising things and changes in the use of smart leadership: there are a lot of ideas among smart people because they feel they can think differently without fear of failure. The human brain is designed to create and

explore in an environment that promotes a sense of security and curiosity.

Flexibility and adaptability A neuroscientist leader not only leads in peacetime, but also develops flexibility in times of crisis. Neuroplasticity, the brain's ability to adapt and change, is activated when people feel positive. This allows organizations to be more flexible in the face of change and uncertainty.

Improve health and job satisfaction Research shows that a work environment based on trust, empathy, and cooperation reduces stress and promotes positive thinking. The human brain responds well to good relationships, which makes people less busy and more satisfied with their work.

Decisions are clear and effective Neuroconscious leaders make decisions very carefully because they understand how stress and emotions affect their brain. This type of leadership is more emotional, less forceful, and more emotional. As a result, smarter and more profitable decisions are made in the long run.

Now: The World Needs Neuroconscious Leaders
This is the deeper truth: the future of leadership is in your hands. Neurowarehouse management is the key to the success of organizations and communities. It is the answer to the problems we face as individuals, groups, companies and countries. It is an antidote to the conflicts, fatigue and tensions that characterize many cultures.

If you want to be part of this revolution, if you want to be a true leader of change, the first step is to develop an awareness of how the human brain works and you can

Page 234

use this knowledge to benefit yourself. Influence your team.

The impact of conscious leadership is not limited to productivity. It's very daring. It can change the health of your colleagues, foster creativity and innovation, and create a cultural shift that affects your organization, the energy of the community, and why not, the entire world.

The Mind of a Leader

FINAL

A compilation of chapters from "The Leader's Brain - Decisions that Impact and Transform", by James Lass

The Leader's Brain - Decisions that Impact and Transform. Decision Making explores the intersection between neuroscience and leadership, demonstrating an understanding of the brain. Strategies can improve leaders' decisions and the impact their leadership has on their teams and organizations. Through a science-based approach to the human brain, Russ provides the necessary tools for leaders who want to make effective decisions, promote healthy workplaces, and achieve sustainable performance.

Below I have organized the main themes of the book and explained them in a scientific yet accessible way to help you apply this knowledge in your life and leadership:

1. The brain as a decision
The beginning of this book emphasizes how the brain is crucial to all the decisions we make in our personal lives. In simpler terms, the brain's job is to make successful decisions, conserve energy, and maximize our lives. However, the way we make decisions is not always clear or logical.

Scientifically we know that the human brain is divided into several areas that work together to make decisions, but emotions often have more influence than we think. The prefrontal cortex, responsible for making rational decisions, can be "altered" by negative or stressful thoughts that activate the amygdala, a part of the brain associated with fear and survival. This can cause a person to make hasty or irrational decisions.

According to Russ, the challenge for leaders is learning to understand and control these brain interactions in order to make informed and appropriate decisions.

2. The importance of mind control
Lass emphasizes that mind control is an important skill for leaders. Leaders who can't control their emotions may make decisions under pressure or due to strong emotions, which can negatively affect their team.

From a neuroscientific perspective, when emotions are not controlled, the brain goes into "survival mode," inhibiting our ability to think rationally. This is especially dangerous for leaders who must make sound decisions in times of great crisis.

Russ teaches that self-control and mental awareness are ways to deal with stress and calm, which leads to effective decision-making. Mindfulness techniques and mind control training are recommended to improve the brain's ability to make decisions.

3. The SCARF model and its effects on leadership
One of the main points of this book is the SCARF model developed by David Rock, which explains how the brain reacts to certain social factors at work. SCARF is an acronym that refers to five things that affect our lives and our work:

S (State): The brain responds to threats and increases state. The feeling of losing or gaining responsibility activates areas of the brain associated with pain or pleasure.

C (Certainty): Uncertainty creates anxiety because the brain tends to predict. Leaders must reduce ambiguity to reduce stress on their teams.

A (Autonomy): Control of the brainstem. Lack of autonomy activates areas of the brain associated with vulnerability. Leaders who foster autonomy and empower their teams activate areas of the brain associated with motivation.

R (Relevance): The brain seeks connection and trusting relationships. The feeling of being "together" in a group activates areas of the brain associated with happiness.

F (Justice): The brain seeks justice. Medical injustice can lead to depression and anxiety, while justice activates brain circuits associated with happiness and harmony.
This model provides leaders with a clear strategy for creating a work environment that fosters motivation, collaboration, and well-being to achieve team productivity and performance.

4. Neuroplasticity and personal growth
Lass also discussed the concept of neuroplasticity, which refers to the brain's ability to remodel itself and adapt to new experiences, learning, and challenges.
In neuroscience, neuroplasticity indicates that the brain is not fixed; This means that leaders can develop new skills and change mindsets that hinder success. For example, the brain can be trained to act calmly in stressful situations or to make sound decisions under pressure.

For leaders, that means it's never too late to fix it. Continuous practice of cognitive and emotional skills, such as decision-making or stress management, can significantly improve the way you manage and make decisions.

5. The role of the social brain in leadership

This book also discusses the concept of the social brain, which refers to how our brain reacts when dealing with other people. Research shows that social relationships and social interaction activate areas of the brain that are important for learning, motivation, and decision-making.

For leaders, this means that engagement and emotional connection with their teams is necessary to create a positive and effective work environment. Leaders who develop relationships of trust and respect activate parts of the brain associated with collaboration and creativity, which help their teams work better together and overcome challenges.

6. Instead of making decisions or decisions based solely on intuition, neurocognitive leaders need to stop, think, and think about everything.

This leadership style helps to avoid biases and cognitive distortions that can affect decisions, such as confirmation bias (looking only for information that confirms our beliefs) or bias (exaggerating initial information that we understand). Smart decision-making also includes the ability to face uncertainty and adapt to new situations.

7. The impact of organizational culture on the brain

Lass examines the impact of organizational culture on employees' brains. A stressful work environment, competition, or lack of support can create chronic stress responses in the brain, leading to decreased performance, energy, and mental health.

In addition, a work culture that promotes mutual respect, cooperation, and employee well-being activates areas of the brain associated with intrinsic health and motivation, creating an environment in which employees feel engaged and productive.

Leaders must recognize the power of leadership culture to change the way their teams think and ultimately improve their performance.

Conclusion:
By understanding how the brain responds to stress, emotions, and relationships, leaders can change their behaviors and strategies to positively impact team performance and well-being.

Lass reminds us that good leadership isn't just about leadership skills or techniques, but about a deep understanding of how decisions and relationships affect people's brains. Leaders who use this neuroscientific approach are better equipped to meet the challenges of today's work environment and transform the way they deliver unique solutions.

Recommended Reading on Neuroscience and Leadership

1. The Frontman's Brain by David Rock

2. *Neuroscience for Leadership* by Jeffrey Schwartz and Sharon Begley

3. Daniel Goleman's Emotional Intelligence

4. David McRaney's Science of Success

5. *Neurocognitive Leadership* of José Luis López Vázquez

6. *The Resonant Leader Creates More* by Richard Boyatzis and Annie McKee

7. John K. Coyle's Neuroscience for Success

8. The Power of the Subconscious Mind by Joseph Murphy

9. *The Organized Mind* by Daniel J. Levitin

10. The Effect of Innovation by Ed Catmull

ABOUT THE AUTHOR

James Lass – NeuroLeadership Coach, Organizational Development, Executive and Business Coach

James began his career in the corporate arena, where he quickly realized the importance of effective leadership and emotional intelligence in organizational success. After several years of experience in team and project management, he decided to redirect his career towards coaching, motivated by his passion for helping others develop their skills and achieve their goals.

Since then, he has worked with a wide variety of clients, ranging from innovative startups to large established corporations. Her approach is client-centric, tailoring her methods and strategies to the specific needs of each individual or team she works with. Her ability to identify and overcome limiting beliefs has been instrumental in her success as a coach, helping her clients overcome obstacles that prevent them from reaching their full potential.

James Lass is one of our most experienced coaches in the field of leadership and organizational, executive and business development. With more than 30 years of experience in large corporations and organizations, James has worked with leaders at all levels, helping them develop their management skills and implement effective strategies for organizational change.

Training and Certifications:
James holds a Bachelor of Computer Science, a business computer scientist as a specialist analyst from TU Dortmund University Dortmund and holds several certifications in Leadership from Harvard Business School online (EdX). In addition, she is certified as a Professional Coach by the World Coaching Corp., International Association of Coaching (IAC) and the Inter-American Confederation of Coaching, she is also a University Professor and External Instructor of the Ministry of Labor and Social Welfare, which supports her commitment to excellence and ethics in her professional practice.

Coaching Approach:
James' work philosophy is based on the belief that leadership is not just about leading others, but about guiding oneself with authenticity and purpose. According to him, an effective leader is one who can inspire his team not only through his technical skills, but through his character, integrity, and vision. For James, developing emotional intelligence is key in this process, as it allows leaders to connect with their team in a deeper and more meaningful way. James uses an integrative approach that combines traditional coaching techniques with modern personal development tools, such as Neuro-Linguistic Programming (NLP) and mindfulness meditation. This combination of approaches allows you to address both the technical and adaptive challenges your customers face, giving them a clear roadmap to success.

Notable Achievements:
James has been instrumental in developing leadership programs at several Fortune 1000 companies, and his clients include world-renowned business leaders. She is known for her ability to identify hidden potential in her clients and guide them towards effective and authentic leadership. Throughout his career, James has helped transform the lives of hundreds of leaders and executives, guiding them on their path to success. His accomplishments include creating highly effective leadership programs that have been implemented in multiple renowned organizations, as well as publishing articles in specialized journals on topics of leadership, emotional intelligence, and personal development. In addition to his coaching work, James is a frequent speaker at conferences and seminars, where he shares his experience and knowledge with a wider audience. Their ability to connect with people and convey their ideas is clear and compelling.

Impact and Recognition:
James' impact on the world of coaching and leadership is undeniable. His clients often highlight his ability to create lasting changes in their lives, both personally and professionally. His empathetic approach and commitment to his clients' success have earned him recognition as one of the top leadership coaches in the industry. In short, James Lass is more than a coach; He is a catalyst for change and a trusted guide for those looking to take their leadership to the next level. His dedication to excellence and passion for personal development continue to inspire leaders around the world to reach new heights in their careers and personal lives.

My Career, Knowledge and Qualifications:
- I am a Life and Transformational Coach at National and International Level, endorsed by the Word Coaching Corp., the International Association of Coaching, the Inter-American Confederation of Coaching, the Ministry of Labor and Social Welfare and Harvard Business School Online
- Business, Executive, Labor, Teambuilding, Communication and Sales Coach.
- I am giving workshops on "Neurosales", "Discover your purpose and passion" and "Leadership Styles" in person and online.
- Solves the problems of: Lack of trust, Internal conflicts, Lack of commitment, Evasion of responsibilities, Lack of focus on results, Communication problems, Poor learning. Use the best approved methodology for Business and improvements in every way. It is an accompaniment with measurable and sustainable results, which is worth the investment in the end!
- I have worked for different universities and schools as well as in colleges as a teacher.
- With more than 30 years of experience in Entrepreneurship, Corporate Organization, Human Resources, Finance, Production, Accounting, Logistics, Warehouses, Purchasing and Sales, Development, Recruitment and more.
- Partner and Co-Founder of Vive Hoy Life Coaching, a company dedicated to Life Transformation.
- With extensive experience in a variety of areas, from business and life coaching to neurosales and leadership workshops, I offer solutions to common problems such as lack of trust, internal conflict, and lack of focus on results. My programs and

accompaniment are designed to generate measurable and sustainable results, providing you with the necessary tools to achieve your goals and overcome any obstacle along the way.

Together with my beautiful wife and the team at Vive Hoy Life Coaching, we are committed to your integral transformation. It's time to take the first step towards a more successful and rewarding life and business!

James Lass